Supporting
Maths

FOR AGES 8–9

Introduction

Supporting Maths is aimed at all those who work with children who have been identified as needing 'additional' or 'different' support in mathematics. It can be used by anyone working with children who fall into this category, whether you are a teacher, classroom assistant or parent.

Typically the eight to nine year-old children for whom the book is intended will be working at the levels expected of Year 2 or Year 3 children or they may simply need extra help in tackling the level of work appropriate for Year 4. Their difficulties may be short term, and overcome with extra practice and support on a one-to-one or small group basis, or they may be long term, where such support enables them to make progress but at a level behind their peer group. The *Record and Review* sheet on page 5 is ideal for keeping track of the targets you set and the progress made by each child.

The 2006 Framework for Teaching Mathematics specifies seven strands of learning:

Strand 1   *Using and applying mathematics*
Strand 2   *Counting and understanding number*
Strand 3   *Knowing and using number facts*
Strand 4   *Calculating*
Strand 5   *Understanding shape*
Strand 6   *Measuring*
Strand 7   *Handling data*

This book addresses all seven strands, drawing on the objectives from Year 2, Year 3 and Year 4. Particular emphasis is placed on understanding number, using number facts and calculating with these. The *Individual record sheet* on page 3 shows the aspects of the seven strands that can be assessed through using the worksheets and through discussion with the pupil.

In this book we provide activities that can be effectively completed on paper, with the help of an adult. The interaction with the adult gives many opportunities for speaking and listening. Explanation by an adult to a child and vice versa provides a firm foundation for mathematical understanding. To reinforce understanding, many activities should be completed in a practical context e.g. children could compare sizes of real objects; they could perform practical addition by combining two groups of objects; they could use base ten equipment to observe the effect of 'crossing tens boundaries'.

Many activities address the key skills of adding and subtracting. Number lines are provided for practical support and lots of tips and suggestions for approaches that are logical and achievable are outlined in the *Notes for teachers* on each page. Year 4 children will also be extending their knowledge of multiplication tables to cover division facts. In this book we provide practice of all the tables from 2 to 10 and link these to division questions. Children need to see that division is closely related to multiplication and that subtraction is closely related to addition. Several worksheets deal with the processes of doubling and halving of numbers. These skills will be useful for children when making estimations of quantities.

However you decide to use these sheets and in whatever context, it is worth remembering that children generally achieve the greatest success in an atmosphere of support and encouragement. Praise from a caring adult can be the best reward for the children's efforts. The worksheets and activities in this book will provide many opportunities for children to enjoy their successes. (As a visual reminder, children can also complete the *My record sheet* on page 4). The development of a positive attitude and the resulting increase in self-esteem will help them with all of their school work and other areas of school life too.

Individual record sheet

Name:

Worksheet	Contents	Teaching and learning objective	Target achieved	Needs more practice
1-10	Addition and subtraction within 20	Strands 1, 2, 3, 4, 6		
11-14	Writing numbers from 1 to over 1000	Strands 1, 2		
15-18	Addition and subtraction of multiples of 10	Strands 1, 2, 3, 4, 6		
19-24	Addition and subtraction 2-digit numbers	Strands 1, 2, 4, 6		
25-26	Subtraction of 2-digit numbers from 100	Strands 1, 2, 3, 4, 6		
27	The 2 times table	Strands 1, 3, 4		
28	The 3 times table	Strands 1, 3, 4		
29	The 4 times table	Strands 1, 3, 4		
30	The 5 times table	Strands 1, 3, 4		
31	The 6 times table	Strands 1, 3, 4		
32	The 7 times table	Strands 1, 3, 4		
33	The 8 times table	Strands 1, 3, 4,		
34	The 9 times table	Strands 1, 3, 4		
35	The 10 times table	Strands 1, 3, 4		
36-38	Division	Strands 1, 3, 4		
39-41	Doubles	Strands 1, 3		
42-43	Halves of numbers	Strands 1, 3, 4		
44	Halves and quarters of shapes	Strand 1, 2		
45	More fractions of shapes	Strands 1, 2		
46	Multiplying by 10	Strands 1, 3, 4		
47	Number sequences	Strands 1, 2, 4		
48	Measuring length	Strands 1, 6		
49	Measuring perimeters of rectangles	Strands 1, 6		
50	Measuring areas of rectangles	Strands 1, 6		
51	Symmetry	Strands 1, 5		
52	Four compass points	Strands 1, 5		
53	Eight compass points	Strands 1, 5		
54	Right angles	Strands 1, 5		
55-57	Venn and Carroll diagrams	Strands 1, 5		
Resource sheets A-B	Shapes for worksheets 55-57	Strands 1, 5		

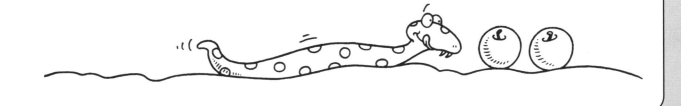

My record sheet

Name: _____   Date of birth: _____

Class: _____   Date: _____

I can...

- select and use suitable equipment and information ☐
- explain decisions, methods and results ☐
- read and write two-digit numbers ☐
- read and write three-digit numbers ☐
- read and write four-digit numbers ☐
- recognise odd and even numbers ☐
- recall all addition and subtraction facts for numbers to 20 ☐
- add and subtract multiples of 10 ☐
- add a one-digit number to any two-digit number ☐
- add a multiple of 10 to any two-digit number ☐
- add a two-digit number to any two-digit number ☐
- subtract a one-digit number from any two-digit number ☐
- subtract a multiple of 10 from any two-digit number ☐
- subtract a two-digit number from a two-digit number ☐
- subtract any two-digit number from 100 ☐
- derive and recall the 2 times table ☐
- derive and recall the 3 times table ☐
- derive and recall the 4 times table ☐
- derive and recall the 5 times table ☐
- derive and recall the 6 times table ☐

- derive and recall the 7 times table ☐
- derive and recall the 8 times table ☐
- derive and recall the 9 times table ☐
- derive and recall the 10 times table ☐
- calculate divisions by using diagrams ☐
- find doubles of numbers from 1 to 10 ☐
- find doubles of multiples of 10 ☐
- find doubles of numbers from 11 to 100 ☐
- find halves of even numbers from 2 to 20 ☐
- find halves of multiples of 10 ☐
- find halves, quarters and three quarters of shapes ☐
- recognise the role of the denominator in a fraction ☐
- recognise the role of the numerator in a fraction ☐
- multiply any number from 1 to 100 by 10 ☐
- continue number sequences with steps of constant size ☐
- measure lengths using standard units ☐
- identify common 2D shapes in different positions ☐
- sort common 2D shapes, referring to their properties ☐
- measure the perimeters of rectangles on a grid ☐
- find the areas of rectangles on a grid ☐
- complete a symmetrical picture ☐
- use the eight compass points to describe direction ☐

Andrew Brodie: Supporting Maths © A & C Black Publishers Ltd. 2007

Record and Review

Name: _____   Date of birth: _____

Teacher: _____   Class: _____

Support assistant: _____

Code of Practice stage: _____   Date targets set: _____

Target

1 _____

2 _____

3 _____

4 _____

Review

Target

1 _____

_____

_____   Target achieved? ☐ Date: _____

2 _____

_____

_____   Target achieved? ☐ Date: _____

3 _____

_____

_____   Target achieved? ☐ Date: _____

4 _____

_____

_____   Target achieved? ☐ Date: _____

Name: _____   **Date:** _____

0   1   2   3   4   5   6   7   8   9   10

How quickly can you answer these questions?

4 + 5 = ☐
7 + 3 = ☐
6 + 4 = ☐
8 + 1 = ☐

3 + 3 = ☐
5 + 2 = ☐
4 + 3 = ☐
3 + 4 = ☐

1 + 5 = ☐
5 + 4 = ☐
7 + 1 = ☐
4 + 4 = ☐

6 + 2 = ☐
3 + 2 = ☐
2 + 4 = ☐
4 + 6 = ☐

3 + 4 = ☐
7 + 2 = ☐
1 + 4 = ☐
4 + 1 = ☐

4 + 2 = ☐
6 + 3 = ☐
8 + 2 = ☐
2 + 8 = ☐

Notes for teachers

Target: Solve one-step problems involving numbers, money or measures, including time; represent the information using numbers or diagrams; identify patterns or relationships involving numbers; describe and explain methods (Strand 1). Read, write and order numbers and position them on a number line (Strand 2). Derive and recall all addition facts for all numbers to at least 10 (Strand 3). Add a one-digit number to a one-digit number (Strand 4). Interpret intervals and divisions on partially numbered scales and record readings accurately; calculate time intervals (Strand 6).

Encourage the child to use the number line, as familiarity with its use will help when s/he meets more difficult questions. Some children choose to use their fingers but watch carefully how they do this as mistakes often happen when a child counts a particular finger more than once! Some children find the questions easier if they use a pencil to move along the line e.g. starting with the pencil on 4 then moving on 5 to find the answer to the first question. Help the child to time her/himself using a clock or watch with a second hand. To make this easier, encourage the child to start each set of questions when the second hand is on twelve. S/he should then record the number of seconds taken, on the clock face provided. This process encourages the child both to observe the small markings on the clock and to work as quickly as possible.

$$0 \quad 1 \quad 2 \quad 3 \quad 4 \quad 5 \quad 6 \quad 7 \quad 8 \quad 9 \quad 10 \quad 11 \quad 12 \quad 13 \quad 14 \quad 15$$

How quickly can you answer these questions?

$3 + 5 = \boxed{}$	$3 + 8 = \boxed{}$	$2 + 2 = \boxed{}$
$4 + 2 = \boxed{}$	$9 + 2 = \boxed{}$	$6 + 4 = \boxed{}$
$1 + 1 = \boxed{}$	$8 + 3 = \boxed{}$	$5 + 3 = \boxed{}$
$7 + 3 = \boxed{}$	$7 + 6 = \boxed{}$	$3 + 4 = \boxed{}$

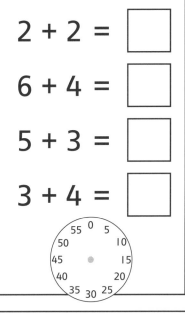

$6 + 8 = \boxed{}$	$5 + 5 = \boxed{}$	$9 + 6 = \boxed{}$
$9 + 4 = \boxed{}$	$8 + 2 = \boxed{}$	$8 + 5 = \boxed{}$
$8 + 4 = \boxed{}$	$1 + 9 = \boxed{}$	$7 + 7 = \boxed{}$
$6 + 6 = \boxed{}$	$6 + 1 = \boxed{}$	$3 + 8 = \boxed{}$

Notes for teachers

Target: Solve one-step problems involving numbers, money or measures, including time; represent the information using numbers or diagrams; identify patterns or relationships involving numbers; describe and explain methods (Strand 1). Read, write and order numbers and position them on a number line (Strand 2). Derive and recall all addition facts for each number to twenty (Strand 3). Add a one-digit number to a one-digit number (Strand 4). Interpret intervals and divisions on partially numbered scales and record readings accurately; calculate time intervals (Strand 6).

Encourage the child to use the number line, as familiarity with its use will help when s/he meets more difficult questions. Help the child to time her/himself using a clock or watch with a second hand. To make this easier, encourage the child to start each set of questions when the second hand is on twelve. S/he should then record the number of seconds taken on the clock face provided. This process encourages the child both to observe the small markings on the clock and to work as quickly as possible. When each set of questions has been answered discuss the answers with the child, encouraging her/him to notice any patterns such as where two questions produce the same answer.

Name: _____ Date: _____

0 1 2 3 4 5 6 7 8 9 10

How quickly can you answer these questions?

9 − 4 = ☐

7 − 3 = ☐

6 − 5 = ☐

8 − 4 = ☐

7 − 2 = ☐

4 − 1 = ☐

9 − 5 = ☐

6 − 5 = ☐

8 − 5 = ☐

6 − 4 = ☐

7 − 3 = ☐

10 − 5 = ☐

3 − 3 = ☐

10 − 7 = ☐

10 − 9 = ☐

8 − 2 = ☐

10 − 4 = ☐

8 − 3 = ☐

6 − 1 = ☐

5 − 3 = ☐

4 − 4 = ☐

6 − 3 = ☐

8 − 4 = ☐

9 − 5 = ☐

Notes for teachers

Target: Solve one-step problems involving numbers, money or measures, including time; represent the information using numbers or diagrams; identify patterns or relationships involving numbers; describe and explain methods (Strand 1). Read, write and order numbers and position them on a number line (Strand 2). Derive and recall all subtraction facts for all numbers to at least 10 (Strand 3). Subtract a one-digit number from a one-digit or two-digit number (Strand 4). Interpret intervals and divisions on partially numbered scales and record readings accurately; calculate time intervals (Strand 6). Encourage the child to use the number line, as familiarity with its use will help when s/he meets more difficult questions. Some children find the questions easier if they use a pencil to move along the line e.g. starting with the pencil on 9 then moving back 4 to find the answer to the first question. Point out that 9 − 4 is not the same as 4 − 9. Help the child to time her/himself using a clock or watch with a second hand. To make this easier, encourage the child to start each set of questions when the second hand is on twelve. S/he should then record the number of seconds taken on the clock face provided. This process encourages the child both to observe the small markings on the clock and to work as quickly as possible. When each set of questions has been answered discuss the answers with the child, encouraging her/him to notice any patterns such as where two questions produce the same answer.

Name: _____   Date: _____

0 1 2 3 4 5 6 7 8 9 10 11 12 13 14 15

How quickly can you answer these questions?

12 − 4 = ☐

13 − 3 = ☐

15 − 5 = ☐

11 − 4 = ☐

11 − 2 = ☐

12 − 5 = ☐

14 − 5 = ☐

13 − 8 = ☐

13 − 5 = ☐

10 − 4 = ☐

12 − 3 = ☐

12 − 5 = ☐

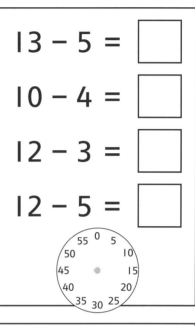

15 − 6 = ☐

15 − 9 = ☐

15 − 8 = ☐

15 − 7 = ☐

12 − 4 = ☐

14 − 3 = ☐

15 − 1 = ☐

13 − 6 = ☐

11 − 7 = ☐

13 − 9 = ☐

14 − 8 = ☐

12 − 7 = ☐

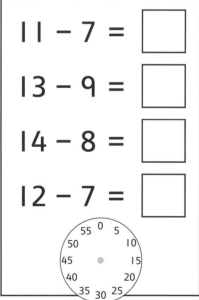

Notes for teachers

Target: Solve one-step problems involving numbers, money or measures, including time; represent the information using numbers or diagrams; identify patterns or relationships involving numbers; describe and explain methods (Strand 1). Read, write and order numbers and position them on a number line (Strand 2). Derive and recall all subtraction facts for all numbers to at least 10 (Strand 3). Subtract a one-digit number from a one-digit or two-digit number (Strand 4). Interpret intervals and divisions on partially numbered scales and record readings accurately; calculate time intervals (Strand 6). Encourage the child to use the number line, as confidence with its use will help the child when he/she meets more difficult questions. Some children find the questions easier if they use a pencil to move along the line e.g. starting with the pencil on 12 then moving back to 4 to find the answer to the first question. Point out that 12 − 4 is not the same as 4 − 12. Help the child to time her/himself using a clock or watch with a second hand. To make this easier, encourage the child to start each set of questions when the second hand is on twelve. S/he should then record the number of seconds taken on the clock face provided. This process encourages the child both to observe the small markings on the clock and to work as quickly as possible. When each set of questions has been answered discuss the answers with the child, encouraging her/him to notice any patterns e.g. 15 − 8 = 7 and 15 − 7 = 8.

Name: _____   **Date:** _____

0   1   2   3   4   5   6   7   8   9   10

How quickly can you answer these questions?

12 + 5 = ☐

14 + 4 = ☐

16 + 1 = ☐

7 + 7 = ☐

13 + 6 = ☐

9 + 5 = ☐

11 + 7 = ☐

8 + 8 = ☐

9 + 6 = ☐

16 + 4 = ☐

8 + 9 = ☐

9 + 9 = ☐

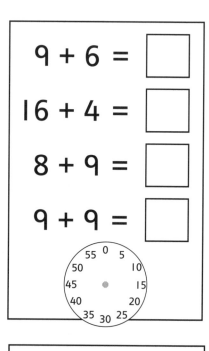

16 + 2 = ☐

9 + 7 = ☐

18 + 2 = ☐

6 + 6 = ☐

13 + 5 = ☐

7 + 2 = ☐

15 + 5 = ☐

10 + 10 = ☐

19 + 1 = ☐

8 + 7 = ☐

12 + 7 = ☐

5 + 5 = ☐

Notes for teachers

Target: Solve one-step problems involving numbers, money or measures, including time; represent the information using numbers or diagrams; identify patterns or relationships involving numbers; describe and explain methods (Strand 1). Read, write and order numbers and position them on a number line (Strand 2). Derive and recall all addition facts for each number to twenty (Strand 3). Add a one-digit number to a one-digit number (Strand 4). Interpret intervals and divisions on partially numbered scales and record readings accurately; calculate time intervals (Strand 6).

Help the child to time her/himself using a clock or watch with a second hand. To make this easier, encourage the child to start each set of questions when the second hand is on twelve. S/he should then record the number of seconds taken on the clock face provided. This process encourages the child both to observe the small markings on the clock and to work as quickly as possible. When each set of questions has been answered discuss the answers with the child, encouraging her/him to notice any patterns such as the fact that the last question in each set is a 'double'.

Name: _____ **Date:** _____

0   1   2   3   4   5   6   7   8   9   10

How quickly can you answer these questions?

20 – 7 = ☐	17 – 6 = ☐	10 – 3 = ☐
18 – 6 = ☐	20 – 2 = ☐	16 – 9 = ☐
12 – 3 = ☐	10 – 8 = ☐	11 – 4 = ☐
14 – 7 = ☐	18 – 9 = ☐	16 – 8 = ☐

12 – 7 = ☐	13 – 8 = ☐	19 – 8 = ☐
13 – 9 = ☐	19 – 6 = ☐	14 – 5 = ☐
18 – 3 = ☐	15 – 1 = ☐	20 – 6 = ☐
20 – 10 = ☐	10 – 5 = ☐	12 – 6 = ☐

Notes for teachers
Target: Solve one-step problems involving numbers, money or measures, including time; represent the information using numbers or diagrams; identify patterns or relationships involving numbers; describe and explain methods (Strand 1). Read, write and order numbers and position them on a number line (Strand 2). Derive and recall all subtraction facts for each number to twenty (Strand 3). Subtract a one-digit number from a two-digit number (Strand 4). Interpret intervals and divisions on partially numbered scales and record readings accurately; calculate time intervals (Strand 6).
Help the child to time her/himself using a clock or watch with a second hand.
When each set of questions has been answered discuss the answers with the child, encouraging her/him to notice any patterns e.g. the answer to the last question in each set has the same value as the number being subtracted. Encourage the child to understand that fourteen subtract seven equals seven because two sevens are fourteen. If you feel that the child is confident you could show her/him that a subtraction question can be completed by 'jumping back' or by 'counting on' e.g. with the question 18 – 6 the child can start at 18 on the number line and 'jump back' 6 to arrive at the answer 12 or start at the 6 and 'count on' 12 places to 18.

Name: _____   **Date:** _____

Look at how we can make 12 by adding numbers together.

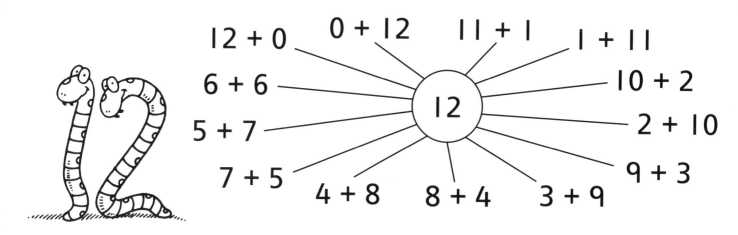

12 + 0   0 + 12   11 + 1   1 + 11

6 + 6   10 + 2

5 + 7   **12**   2 + 10

7 + 5   9 + 3

4 + 8   8 + 4   3 + 9

Find ways of making 13.

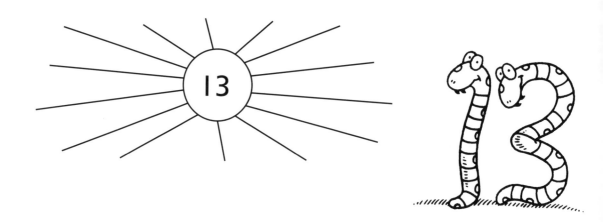

13

Notes for teachers

Target: Solve one-step problems involving numbers; represent the information using numbers or diagrams; identify patterns or relationships involving numbers; describe and explain methods (Strand 1). Read, write and order numbers; count on from and back to zero (Strand 2). Derive and recall all addition facts for each number to twenty (Strand 3). Add a one-digit number to a one-digit or a two-digit number (Strand 4).

Discuss the example of number 12 with the child. Point out that all the number bonds use whole numbers. At this stage we are not looking at fractions and we are not splitting the number into more than two parts. Some children find it helpful to use counters or blocks, observing how the number can be split into two parts. Encourage the child to notice that each pair of numbers appears twice e.g. 9 + 3 and 3 + 9, except for 6 + 6 because 6 is half of 12. After the child has looked closely at the number bonds for 12, support her/him in discovering the bonds for 13, then for 14. You may like to continue this activity on separate sheets of paper, helping the child to find bonds for 15, 16, 17, 18, 19 and 20.

Name: Date:

0 1 2 3 4 5 6 7 8 9 10 11 12 13 14 15 16 17 18 19 20

How many questions can you answer in one minute?

There are sixty seconds
in one minute.
There are sixty minutes
in one hour.

12 + 7 = ☐	9 + 9 = ☐	11 + 1 = ☐
9 + 6 = ☐	12 + 3 = ☐	8 + 6 = ☐
11 + 1 = ☐	16 + 4 = ☐	13 + 7 = ☐
17 + 2 = ☐	6 + 7 = ☐	12 + 5 = ☐
13 + 5 = ☐	18 + 2 = ☐	9 + 5 = ☐
15 + 3 = ☐	11 + 6 = ☐	7 + 5 = ☐
8 + 7 = ☐	8 + 5 = ☐	15 + 4 = ☐
6 + 8 = ☐	7 + 7 = ☐	6 + 6 = ☐
14 + 4 = ☐	14 + 5 = ☐	18 + 1 = ☐
8 + 4 = ☐	10 + 10 = ☐	17 + 3 = ☐

Notes for teachers

Target: Solve one-step problems involving numbers, money or measures, including time; represent the information using numbers or diagrams; identify patterns or relationships involving numbers; describe and explain methods (Strand 1). Read, write and order numbers and position them on a number line (Strand 2). Derive and recall all addition facts for each number to twenty (Strand 3). Add a one-digit number to a one-digit or two-digit number (Strand 4). Interpret intervals and divisions on partially numbered scales and record readings accurately; calculate time intervals (Strand 6).

Discuss the picture of the clock with the child, reminding her/him that sixty seconds make one minute and that sixty minutes make one hour. Encourage her/him to complete as many questions as possible from the first column in exactly one minute. At the end of the minute mark the answers with the child, discussing any mistakes that have been made. Give lots of praise for the child's success in both accuracy and quantity then move on to the next column of questions. Repeated practice is a good way of building children's confidence in their number work.

Name: Date:

0 1 2 3 4 5 6 7 8 9 10 11 12 13 14 15 16 17 18 19 20

How many questions can you answer in one minute?

There are sixty seconds
in one minute.
There are sixty minutes
in one hour.

$12 - 6 =$	$20 - 12 =$	$16 - 8 =$
$19 - 3 =$	$12 - 3 =$	$7 - 5 =$
$8 - 5 =$	$16 - 9 =$	$13 - 7 =$
$20 - 9 =$	$9 - 5 =$	$14 - 7 =$
$9 - 7 =$	$18 - 7 =$	$9 - 9 =$
$15 - 9 =$	$11 - 6 =$	$18 - 11 =$
$11 - 8 =$	$8 - 3 =$	$15 - 8 =$
$14 - 9 =$	$17 - 9 =$	$11 - 2 =$
$18 - 9 =$	$14 - 5 =$	$20 - 10 =$
$10 - 10 =$	$13 - 8 =$	$17 - 8 =$

Notes for teachers

Target: Solve one-step problems involving numbers, money or measures, including time; represent the information using numbers or diagrams; identify patterns or relationships involving numbers; describe and explain methods (Strand 1). Read, write and order numbers and position them on a number line (Strand 2). Derive and recall all subtraction facts for each number to twenty (Strand 3). Subtract a one-digit or two-digit number from a one-digit or two-digit number (Strand 4). Interpret intervals and divisions on partially numbered scales and record readings accurately; calculate time intervals (Strand 6). Discuss the picture of the clock with the child, reminding her/him that sixty seconds make one minute and that sixty minutes make one hour. Encourage her/him to complete as many questions as possible from the first column in exactly one minute. At the end of the minute mark the answers with the child, discussing any mistakes that have been made. Give lots of praise for the child's success in both accuracy and quantity before moving on to the next column of questions. Repeated practice is a good way of building children's confidence in their number work.

0 1 2 3 4 5 6 7 8 9 10 11 12 13 14 15 16 17 18 19 20

How many questions can you answer in one minute?

There are sixty seconds
in one minute.
There are sixty minutes
in one hour.

8 + 6 =	15 − 9 =	11 + 4 =
9 − 5 =	12 + 6 =	20 − 8 =
12 + 7 =	16 − 4 =	6 + 6 =
13 + 6 =	15 + 4 =	13 − 5 =
18 − 9 =	20 − 7 =	15 − 8 =
10 − 8 =	9 + 6 =	7 + 8 =
12 − 9 =	8 − 6 =	16 − 9 =
7 + 7 =	11 + 7 =	8 + 8 =
14 + 6 =	14 − 5 =	18 − 9 =
20 − 4 =	2 + 12 =	17 − 8 =

Notes for teachers

Target: Solve one-step problems involving numbers, money or measures, including time; represent the information using numbers or diagrams; identify patterns or relationships involving numbers; describe and explain methods (Strand 1). Read, write and order numbers and position them on a number line (Strand 2). Derive and recall all addition and subtraction facts for each number to twenty (Strand 3). Add or subtract mentally combinations of one-digit and two-digit numbers (Strand 4). Interpret intervals and divisions on partially numbered scales and record readings accurately; calculate time intervals (Strand 6). Discuss the picture of the clock with the child, reminding her/him that sixty seconds make one minute and that sixty minutes make one hour. Explain that the questions on this page include additions and subtractions and that s/he will need to look carefully at the sign in each question. Encourage her/him to complete as many questions as possible from the first column in exactly one minute. At the end of the minute mark the answers with the child, discussing any mistakes that have been made. Give lots of praise for the child's success in both accuracy and quantity before moving on to the next column of questions. Repeated practice is a good way of building children's confidence in their number work.

Name: _____   **Date:** _____

This number is eighty-three:

tens   units

8   3

Listen to your teacher. Write the numbers.

[grid of empty answer boxes: three rows of 7, 7 and 6 boxes]

Notes for teachers

Target: Identify patterns and relationships involving numbers (Strand 1). Read, write and order whole numbers to at least 1000 (Strand 2).

You may decide to cut off or hide these teacher's notes so that the child cannot see the numbers that you are going to dictate. Ask the child to look carefully at the number 83, pointing out that the 8 is in the tens column and the 3 is in the units column. You could ask the child to draw rings around the stars to arrange them into groups of ten. There will, of course, be eight groups of ten plus three extra stars. When the child is ready, dictate the following numbers to her/him:

| 17 | 45 | 93 | 38 | 70 | 67 | 82 | 21 | 56 | 99 |
| 8 | 97 | 50 | 29 | 51 | 26 | 32 | 84 | 77 | 100 |

For most pupils this will be a very simple activity but it provides a good introduction to the more difficult numbers they will encounter on Worksheets 12, 13 and 14.

Name: _____ **Date:** _____

This number is two hundred and forty seven:

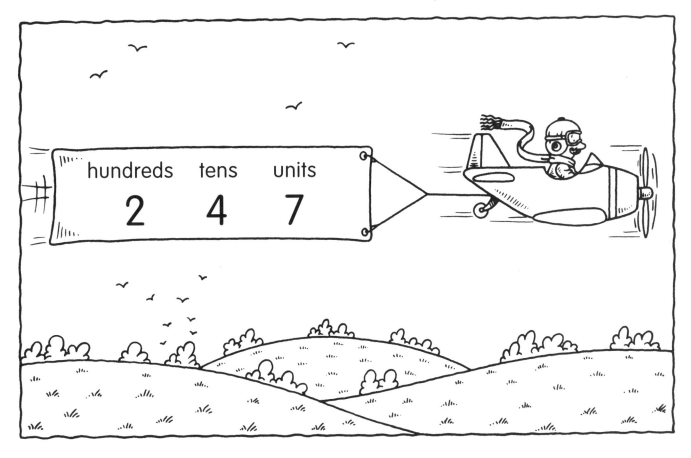

hundreds	tens	units
2	4	7

Listen to your teacher. Write the numbers.

[ ] [ ] [ ] [ ] [ ] [ ] [ ]

[ ] [ ] [ ] [ ] [ ] [ ] [ ]

[ ] [ ] [ ] [ ] [ ] [ ] [ ]

Notes for teachers

Target: Identify patterns and relationships involving numbers (Strand 1). Read, write and order whole numbers to at least 1000 (Strand 2).

You may decide to cut off/hide these teacher's notes so that the child cannot see the numbers that you are going to dictate. Ask the child to look carefully at the number 247, pointing out that the 2 is in the hundreds column, the 4 is in the tens column and the 7 is in the units column. When the child is ready, dictate the following numbers to her/him:

413   678   329   504   817   444   794   800   965   113
209   483   699   722   935   215   857   285   541   902

Watch carefully how the child writes each number and correct any misunderstandings. Numbers such as 504 and 209 often cause difficulty for children and may need to be discussed. You could extend the activity by asking questions such as: 'What is one more than six hundred and ninety-nine?' 'What is one less than eight hundred?'

Andrew Brodie: Supporting Maths © A & C Black Publishers Ltd. 2007

Name: _____

Date: _____

This number is four thousand and eighteen:

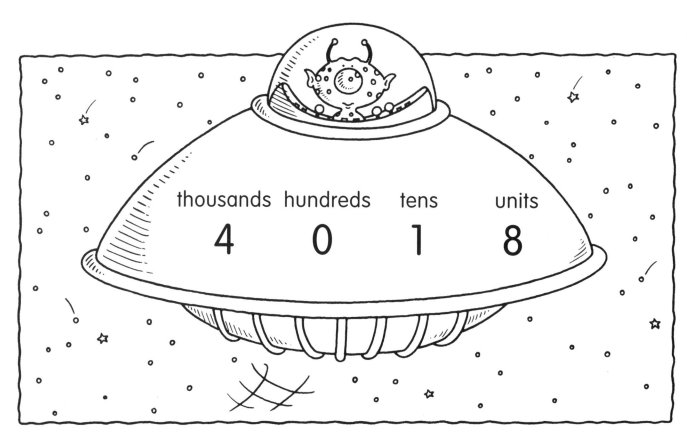

thousands	hundreds	tens	units
4	0	1	8

Listen to your teacher. Write the numbers.

Notes for teachers

Target: Identify patterns and relationships involving numbers (Strand 1). Read, write and order whole numbers to at least 1000 (Strand 2).

You may decide to cut off/hide these teacher's notes so that the child cannot see the numbers that you are going to dictate. Ask the child to look carefully at the number 4018, pointing out that the 4 is in the thousands column, the 0 is in the hundreds column because there are no hundreds in this particular number, the 1 is in the tens column and the 8 is in the units column. When the child is ready, dictate the following numbers:

2534 1798 5004 3692 6845 9221 4983 7288 5369 2323
8742 5604 9067 3259 9408 5581 2365 1947 2006 4444

Watch carefully how the child writes each number and correct any misunderstandings. Many children have misconceptions about 'big numbers'.

Name: _____ **Date:** _____

This number is seven thousand:

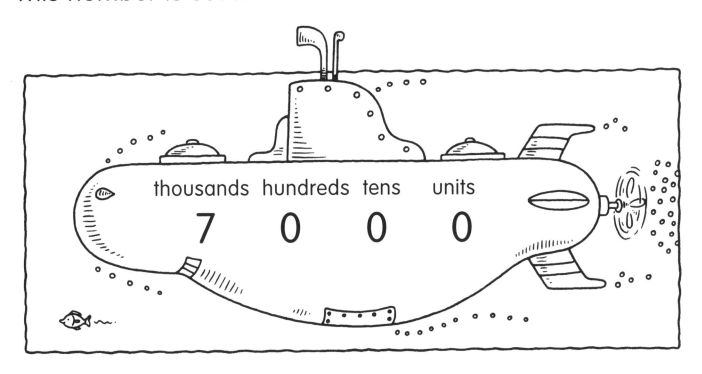

thousands	hundreds	tens	units
7	0	0	0

Listen to your teacher. Write the numbers.

Notes for teachers

Target: Identify patterns and relationships involving numbers (Strand 1). Read, write and order whole numbers to at least 1000 (Strand 2).

You may decide to cut off/hide these teacher's notes so that the child cannot see the numbers that you are going to dictate. Ask the child to look carefully at the number 7000, pointing out that the 7 is in the thousands column, the 0 is in the hundreds column because there are no hundreds in this particular number, the 0 is in the tens column because there are no tens in this particular number, and the 0 is in the units column because there are no units in this particular number. When the child is ready, dictate the following numbers:

8000	2400	369	800	80	5900	6400	2000	7114	99
1496	700	3200	5000	904	4000	6006	1001	214	9090

Watch carefully how the child writes each number and correct any misunderstandings. Many children have misconceptions about 'big numbers'.

Name: _____

Date: _____

Work with your teacher to answer these questions.

30 + 20 = ☐   40 + 40 = ☐

70 + 20 = ☐   90 + 10 = ☐

80 + 10 = ☐   20 + 10 = ☐

50 + 30 = ☐   10 + 40 = ☐

50 + 40 = ☐   50 + 50 = ☐

60 + 30 = ☐   30 + 30 = ☐

100
90
80
70
60
50
40
30
20
10
0

Notes for teachers

Target: Solve one-step problems involving numbers, money or measures, including time; represent the information using numbers or diagrams; identify patterns or relationships involving numbers; describe and explain methods (Strand 1). Read, write and order numbers Nand position them on a number line (Strand 2). Derive and recall sums and differences of multiples of ten (Strand 3). Add a two-digit number to a two-digit number (Strand 4). Interpret intervals and divisions on partially numbered scales and record readings accurately (Strand 6).

Help the child use the number line to answer these questions. Check that s/he understands that the number line is only marked with the multiples of ten but that the other numbers can be found by counting the markers between the tens. So, as an extension activity, you could ask the child to mark on the positions of numbers that you specify e.g. 6, 47, 93. Repeated practice is a good way of building children's confidence in their number work.

Name: _____ **Date:** _____

Work with your teacher to answer these questions.

90 + 20 = ☐   50 + 30 = ☐

70 + 40 = ☐   90 + 80 = ☐

60 + 70 = ☐   80 + 90 = ☐

50 + 60 = ☐   100 + 60 = ☐

80 + 40 = ☐   70 + 70 = ☐

80 + 70 = ☐   90 + 90 = ☐

200
180
160
140
120
100
80
60
40
20
0

Notes for teachers
Target: Solve one-step problems involving numbers, money or measures, including time; represent the information using numbers or diagrams; identify patterns or relationships involving numbers; describe and explain methods (Strand 1). Read, write and order numbers and position them on a number line (Strand 2). Derive and recall sums and differences of multiples of ten (Strand 3). Add a two-digit number to a two-digit number (Strand 4). Interpret intervals and divisions on partially numbered scales and record readings accurately (Strand 6).
Help the child use the number line to answer these questions; check that s/he understands that the number line is only marked with the multiples of ten but that the other numbers can be found by counting the markers between the tens. So, as an extension activity, you could ask the child to mark on the positions of numbers that you specify: for example, 9, 75, 128. Note that most of the questions on this sheet involve 'crossing the hundreds boundary'. Encourage the child to notice the links between simpler questions and the questions on this sheet, e.g. 8 + 4 = 12 and 80 + 40 = 120. Repeated practice is a good way of building children's confidence in their number work.

Name:

Date:

Work with your teacher to answer these questions.

$90 - 20 =$ ☐ $100 - 80 =$ ☐

$40 - 40 =$ ☐ $50 - 30 =$ ☐

$60 - 50 =$ ☐ $100 - 60 =$ ☐

$80 - 30 =$ ☐ $80 - 40 =$ ☐

$90 - 40 =$ ☐ $50 - 20 =$ ☐

$70 - 60 =$ ☐ $90 + 70 =$ ☐

100
90
80
70
60
50
40
30
20
10
0

Notes for teachers
Target: Solve one-step problems involving numbers, money or measures, including time; represent the information using numbers or diagrams; identify patterns or relationships involving numbers; describe and explain methods (Strand 1). Read, write and order numbers Nand position them on a number line (Strand 2). Derive and recall sums Date differences of multiples of ten (Strand 3). Subtract a two-digit number from a two-digit number (Strand 4). Interpret intervals and divisions on partially numbered scales and record readings accurately (Strand 6).
Help the child use the number line to answer these questions; check that s/he understands that the number line is only marked with the multiples of ten but that the other numbers can be found by counting the markers between the tens. So, as an extension activity, you could ask the child to mark on the positions of numbers that you specify e.g. 17, 39, 81. Repeated practice is a good way of building children's confidence in their number work.

Work with your teacher to
answer these questions.

$110 - 20 = \square$ $90 - 60 = \square$

$160 - 70 = \square$ $150 - 70 = \square$

$150 - 30 = \square$ $190 - 80 = \square$

$180 - 90 = \square$ $140 + 70 = \square$

$200 - 40 = \square$ $160 - 80 = \square$

$170 - 80 = \square$ $120 - 60 = \square$

200 —
180 —
160 —
140 —
120 —
100 —
80 —
60 —
40 —
20 —
0 —

Notes for teachers

Target: Solve one-step problems involving numbers, money or measures, including time; represent the information using numbers or diagrams; identify patterns or relationships involving numbers; describe and explain methods (Strand 1). Read, write and order numbers and position them on a number line (Strand 2). Derive and recall sums and differences of multiples of ten (Strand 3). Subtract a two-digit number from a two-digit number (Strand 4). Interpret intervals and divisions on partially numbered scales and record readings accurately (Strand 6).

Help the child use the number line to answer these questions; check that s/he understands that the number line is only marked with the multiples of ten but that the other numbers can be found by counting the markers between the tens. So, as an extension activity, you could ask the child to mark on the positions of numbers that you specify e.g. 43, 128, 199. Note that most of the questions on this sheet involve 'crossing the hundreds boundary'. Repeated practice is a good way of building children's confidence in their number work.

worksheet
19

Name: Date:

Addition of one-digit numbers to two-digit numbers

Work with your teacher to answer these questions.

37 + 6 = ☐   47 + 7 = ☐

43 + 2 = ☐   91 + 9 = ☐

59 + 7 = ☐   84 + 8 = ☐

74 + 9 = ☐   67 + 4 = ☐

23 + 7 = ☐   78 + 9 = ☐

12 + 9 = ☐   37 + 8 = ☐

100
90
80
70
60
50
40
30
20
10
0

Notes for teachers

Target: Solve one-step problems involving numbers, money or measures, including time; represent the information using numbers or diagrams; identify patterns or relationships involving numbers; describe and explain methods (Strand 1). Read, write and order numbers and position them on a number line (Strand 2). Add a one-digit number to a two-digit number (Strand 4). Interpret intervals and divisions on partially numbered scales and record readings accurately (Strand 6). Help the child use the number line to answer these questions. Check that s/he understands that the number line is only marked with the multiples of ten but that the other numbers can be found by counting the markers between the tens e.g. for the first question help the child to find the correct position of 37 then to count on 6 places. Repeated practice is a good way of building children's confidence in their number work.

     Andrew Brodie: Supporting Maths © A & C Black Publishers Ltd. 2007

Name: _____   **Date:** _____

Work with your teacher to
answer these questions.

47 + 16 = ☐   28 + 14 = ☐

23 + 12 = ☐   47 + 18 = ☐

84 + 15 = ☐   36 + 14 = ☐

51 + 19 = ☐   54 + 13 = ☐

37 + 17 = ☐   78 + 16 = ☐

73 + 19 = ☐   26 + 18 = ☐

```
100
 90
 80
 70
 60
 50
 40
 30
 20
 10
  0
```

Notes for teachers

Target: Solve one-step problems involving numbers, money or measures, including time; represent the information using numbers or diagrams; identify patterns or relationships involving numbers; describe and explain methods (Strand 1). Read, write and order numbers and position them on a number line (Strand 2). Add a two-digit number to a two-digit number (Strand 4). Interpret intervals and divisions on partially numbered scales Dand record readings accurately (Strand 6).
Help the child use the number line to answer these questions. Check that s/he understands that the number line is only marked with the multiples of ten but that the other numbers can be found by counting the markers between the tens e.g. for the first question help the child to find the correct position of 47 then to add on 16. If you feel that the child is confident, show her/him that the adding on can be completed in two parts. S/he could 'jump on' 10 to reach 57 then count on the extra 6 to reach the answer 63. Then show her/him that s/he could count on the 6 units first to reach 53 then jump on 10 to reach 63. Repeated practice is a good way of building children's confidence in their number work.

Name: _____

Date: _____

Addition of two-digit numbers to two-digit numbers

Work with your teacher to answer these questions.

37 + 6 = ☐

43 + 2 = ☐

59 + 7 = ☐

74 + 9 = ☐

23 + 7 = ☐

12 + 9 = ☐

47 + 7 = ☐

91 + 9 = ☐

84 + 8 = ☐

67 + 4 = ☐

78 + 9 = ☐

37 + 8 = ☐

100
90
80
70
60
50
40
30
20
10
0

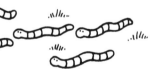

Notes for teachers
Target: Solve one-step problems involving numbers, money or measures, including time; represent the information using numbers or diagrams; identify patterns or relationships involving numbers; describe and explain methods (Strand 1). Read, write and order numbers and position them on a number line (Strand 2). Add a two-digit number to a two-digit number (Strand 4). Interpret intervals and divisions on partially numbered scales and record readings accurately (Strand 6).
Help the child use the number line to answer these questions. Check that s/he understands that the number line is only marked with the multiples of ten but that the other numbers can be found by counting the markers between the tens e.g. for the first question help the child to find the correct position of 47 then to add on 36. Show her/him that the adding on can be completed in two parts. S/he could 'jump on' 30 to reach 77 then count on the extra 6 units to reach the answer 83. Then show her/him that s/he could count on the 6 units first to reach 53 then jump on 30 to reach 83. Note that the last question extends just beyond the number line. Observe how the child copes with this. If s/he can complete the question successfully s/he is developing good numerical skills. Repeated practice is a good way of building children's confidence in their number.

Name: _____ **Date:** _____

worksheet
22

Work with your teacher to answer these questions.

$52 - 4 =$ ☐ $85 - 9 =$ ☐

$49 - 8 =$ ☐ $46 - 8 =$ ☐

$83 - 7 =$ ☐ $72 - 4 =$ ☐

$91 - 5 =$ ☐ $22 - 8 =$ ☐

$62 - 4 =$ ☐ $34 - 9 =$ ☐

$31 - 4 =$ ☐ $93 - 7 =$ ☐

100
90
80
70
60
50
40
30
20
10
0

Notes for teachers
Target: Solve one-step problems involving numbers, money or measures, including time; represent the information using numbers or diagrams; identify patterns or relationships involving numbers; describe and explain methods (Strand 1). Read, write and order numbers and position them on a number line (Strand 2). Subtract a one-digit number from a two-digit number (Strand 4). Interpret intervals and divisions on partially numbered scales and record readings accurately (Strand 6). Help the child use the number line to answer these questions. Check that s/he understands that the number line is only marked with the multiples of ten but that the other numbers can be found by counting the markers between the tens e.g. for the first question help the child to find the correct position of 52 then to count back 4 places. Encourage the child to notice any patterns or similarities. Note, for example, that the first question in each column is structured in the same way. Repeated practice is a good way of building children's confidence in their number work.

Andrew Brodie: Supporting Maths © A & C Black Publishers Ltd. 2007

Name: _____   **Date:** _____

Work with your teacher to answer these questions.

63 − 17 = ☐   52 − 15 = ☐

41 − 13 = ☐   64 − 12 = ☐

92 − 14 = ☐   83 − 17 = ☐

85 − 16 = ☐   42 − 19 = ☐

73 − 17 = ☐   91 − 12 = ☐

90 − 16 = ☐   100 − 14 = ☐

100
90
80
70
60
50
40
30
20
10
0

Notes for teachers

Target: Solve one-step problems involving numbers, money or measures, including time; represent the information using numbers or diagrams; identify patterns or relationships involving numbers; describe and explain methods (Strand 1). Read, write and order numbers and position them on a number line (Strand 2). Subtract a two-digit number from a two-digit number (Strand 4). Interpret intervals and divisions on partially numbered scales and record readings accurately (Strand 6). Help the child use the number line to answer these questions. Check that s/he understands that the number line is only marked with the multiples of ten but that the other numbers can be found by counting the markers between the tens e.g. for the first question help the child to find the correct position of 63 then to subtract 17. S/he could jump back 10 to reach 53 then count back the extra 7 units to reach the answer 46. Then show her/him that s/he could instead count back the 7 units first to reach 56 then jump back 10 to reach 46. Repeated practice is a good way of building children's confidence in their number work.

Andrew Brodie: Supporting Maths © A & C Black Publishers Ltd. 2007

Name: _____   **Date:** _____

Work with your teacher to
answer these questions.

77 − 29 = ☐   53 − 25 = ☐

46 − 28 = ☐   50 − 25 = ☐

95 − 37 = ☐   97 − 49 = ☐

100 − 64 = ☐   74 − 38 = ☐

87 − 39 = ☐   82 − 35 = ☐

80 − 26 = ☐   100 − 49 = ☐

100
90
80
70
60
50
40
30
20
10
0

Notes for teachers

Target: Solve one-step problems involving numbers, money or measures, including time; represent the information using numbers or diagrams; identify patterns or relationships involving numbers; describe and explain methods (Strand 1). Read, write and order numbers and position them on a number line (Strand 2). Subtract a two-digit number from a two-digit number (Strand 4). Interpret intervals and divisions on partially numbered scales and record readings accurately (Strand 6). Help the child use the number line to answer these questions. Check that s/he understands that the number line is only marked with the multiples of ten but that the other numbers can be found by counting the markers between the tens e.g. for the first question help the child to find the correct position of 77 then to subtract 29. S/he could jump back 20 to reach 57 then count back the extra 9 units to reach the answer 48. Then show her/him that s/he could instead count back the 9 units first to reach 68 then jump back 20 to reach 48. Repeated practice is a good way of building children's confidence in their number work.

worksheet 25

Name: _____   **Date:** _____

Work with your teacher to answer these questions.

100 − 50 = ☐   100 − 20 = ☐

100 − 40 = ☐   100 − 0 = ☐

100 − 70 = ☐   100 − 90 = ☐

100 − 100 = ☐   100 − 80 = ☐

100 − 60 = ☐   100 − 10 = ☐

100 − 30 = ☐   100 − 1 = ☐

Number line scale: 100, 90, 80, 70, 60, 50, 40, 30, 20, 10, 0

Notes for teachers

Target: Solve one-step problems involving numbers, money or measures, including time; represent the information using numbers or diagrams; identify patterns or relationships involving numbers; describe and explain methods (Strand 1). Read, write and order numbers and position them on a number line (Strand 2). Derive and recall number pairs that total 100 (Strand 3). Subtract a two-digit number from 100 (Strand 4). Interpret intervals and divisions on partially numbered scales and record readings accurately (Strand 6).

Help the child use the number line to answer these questions. Check that s/he understands that the number line is only marked with the multiples of ten but that the other numbers can be found by counting the markers between the tens. With these questions you could show the child that we can jump on or count on from the smaller number until we reach 100 or we can start at 100 and jump back or count back. Repeated practice is a good way of building children's confidence in their number work.

    Andrew Brodie: Supporting Maths © A & C Black Publishers Ltd. 2007

Name: _____ **Date:** _____

worksheet
26

Work with your teacher to
answer these questions.

100 − 33 = ☐   100 − 50 = ☐

100 − 46 = ☐   100 − 18 = ☐

100 − 51 = ☐   100 − 52 = ☐

100 − 99 = ☐   100 − 48 = ☐

100 − 67 = ☐   100 − 53 = ☐

100 − 33 = ☐   100 − 47 = ☐

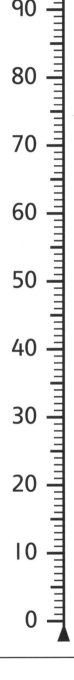

100
90
80
70
60
50
40
30
20
10
0

Notes for teachers

Target: Solve one-step problems involving numbers, money or measures, including time; represent the information using numbers or diagrams; identify patterns or relationships involving numbers; describe and explain methods (Strand 1). Read, write and order numbers and position them on a number line (Strand 2). Derive and recall number pairs that total 100 (Strand 3). Subtract a two-digit number from 100 (Strand 4). Interpret intervals and divisions on partially numbered scales and record readings accurately (Strand 6).

Help the child use the number line to answer these questions. Check that s/he understands that the number line is only marked with the multiples of ten but that the other numbers can be found by counting the markers between the tens. With these questions you could show the child that we can jump on or count on from the smaller number until we reach 100 or we can start at 100 and jump back or count back. Many children make mistakes when subtracting from 100, particularly when they are beginning to gain confidence e.g. they are likely to give the answer 77 to the first question as they know that 100 − 30 = 70 and that 10 − 3 = 7: using the number line effectively can overcome this problem. Repeated practice is a good way of building children's confidence in their number work.

How many squares do you think there are here?

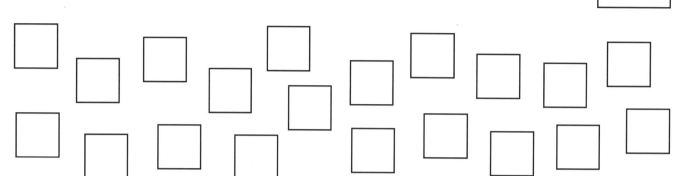

Now count the squares.

Draw rings around groups of two squares. Use these groups to help you to fill in the two times table.

1 x 2 = ☐ ------------------   6 x 2 = ☐ ------------------

2 x 2 = ☐ ------------------   7 x 2 = ☐ ------------------

3 x 2 = ☐ ------------------   8 x 2 = ☐ ------------------

4 x 2 = ☐ ------------------   9 x 2 = ☐ ------------------

5 x 2 = ☐ ------------------   10 x 2 = ☐ ------------------

Notes for teachers
Target: Solve one-step problems involving numbers, money or measures, including time; represent the information using numbers or diagrams; make and use tables to organise and interpret information; identify patterns or relationships involving numbers; describe and explain methods (Strand 1). Derive and recall multiplication facts; recognise multiples of 2 up to 1000 (Strand 3). Multiply one-digit numbers by 10 (Strand 4).
There are several aspects to the work on this page: sensible estimation; accurate counting; making the two times table; observing the effect of multiplying by ten. The child may need help in all these areas. Note that many children have difficulty with accurate counting and can be shown that the strategy of grouping in twos can make the process easier. Once the table is complete discuss any patterns e.g. all the answers are even numbers; the numbers 2, 4, 6, 8 and 0 all appear in the units column twice. Pay particular attention to 10 x 2 = 20. Point out that the number 2 in the answer is sitting in the tens column and that there is a 0 in the units column for that number. You could extend the activity by showing the child numbers such as 94, which must be a multiple of two because it ends in a four. If the child is gaining confidence you could suggest that s/he uses a calculator to find how many twos are in ninety-four. This introduces a link between multiplication and division: 94 ÷ 2 = 47 because 47 x 2 = 94. You could continue this activity by showing numbers such as 518, 836, 480, etc, and by asking questions such as 'is 999 a multiple of two?' and explaining that it cannot be because it does not have a two, four, six, eight or zero in the units column.

Name: _____   **Date:** _____

How many triangles do
you think there are here?

Now count the triangles.

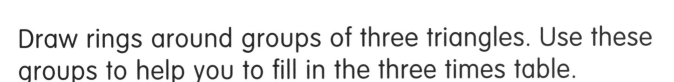

Draw rings around groups of three triangles. Use these
groups to help you to fill in the three times table.

1 x 3 = ☐ _ _ _ _ _ _ _ _ _ _ _ _ _ _   6 x 3 = ☐ _ _ _ _ _ _ _ _ _ _ _ _ _ _

2 x 3 = ☐ _ _ _ _ _ _ _ _ _ _ _ _ _ _   7 x 3 = ☐ _ _ _ _ _ _ _ _ _ _ _ _ _ _

3 x 3 = ☐ _ _ _ _ _ _ _ _ _ _ _ _ _ _   8 x 3 = ☐ _ _ _ _ _ _ _ _ _ _ _ _ _ _

4 x 3 = ☐ _ _ _ _ _ _ _ _ _ _ _ _ _ _   9 x 3 = ☐ _ _ _ _ _ _ _ _ _ _ _ _ _ _

5 x 3 = ☐ _ _ _ _ _ _ _ _ _ _ _ _ _ _   10 x 3 = ☐ _ _ _ _ _ _ _ _ _ _ _ _ _ _

Notes for teachers
Target: Solve one-step problems involving numbers, money or measures, including time; represent the information using numbers or diagrams; make and use tables to organise and interpret information; identify patterns or relationships involving numbers; describe and explain methods (Strand 1). Derive and recall multiplication facts (Strand 3). Multiply one-digit numbers by 10 (Strand 4).
There are several aspects to the work on this page: sensible estimation; accurate counting; making the three times table; observing the effect of multiplying by ten. The child may need help in all these areas. Note that many children have difficulty with accurate counting and can be shown that the strategy of grouping in threes can make the process easier. Once the table is complete discuss any patterns e.g. some answers are even, some are odd. Can the child see why? Pay particular attention to 10 x 3 = 30. Point out that the number 3 in the answer is sitting in the tens column and that there is a 0 in the units column for that number.

Name:

Date:

How many rectangles do
you think there are here?

Now count the rectangles.

Draw rings around groups of four rectangles. Use these
groups to help you to fill in the four times table.

1 x 4 =	6 x 4 =
2 x 4 =	7 x 4 =
3 x 4 =	8 x 4 =
4 x 4 =	9 x 4 =
5 x 4 =	10 x 4 =

Notes for teachers

Target: Solve one-step problems involving numbers, money or measures, including time; represent the information using numbers or diagrams; make and use tables to organise and interpret information; identify patterns or relationships involving numbers; describe and explain methods (Strand 1). Derive and recall multiplication facts (Strand 3). Multiply one-digit numbers by 10 (Strand 4).

There are several aspects to the work on this page: sensible estimation; accurate counting; making the four times table; observing the effect of multiplying by ten. The child may need help in all these areas. Note that many children have difficulty with accurate counting and can be shown that the strategy of grouping in fours can make the process easier. Once the table is complete discuss any patterns e.g. all the answers are even numbers. Pay particular attention to 10 x 4 = 40. Point out that the number 4 in the answer is sitting in the tens column and that there is a 0 in the units column for that number.

Name: **Date:**

How many pentagons do
you think there are here?

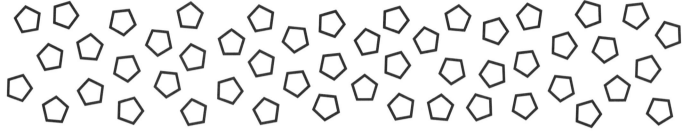

Now count the pentagons.

Draw rings around groups of five pentagons. Use these
groups to help you to fill in the five times table.

1 x 5 = ☐ _____   6 x 5 = ☐ _____

2 x 5 = ☐ _____   7 x 5 = ☐ _____

3 x 5 = ☐ _____   8 x 5 = ☐ _____

4 x 5 = ☐ _____   9 x 5 = ☐ _____

5 x 5 = ☐ _____   10 x 5 = ☐ _____

Notes for teachers

Target: Solve one-step problems involving numbers, money or measures, including time; represent the information using numbers or diagrams; make and use tables to organise and interpret information; identify patterns or relationships involving numbers; describe and explain methods (Strand 1). Derive and recall multiplication facts; recognise multiples of 5 up to 1000 (Strand 3). Multiply one-digit numbers by 10 (Strand 4).

There are several aspects to the work on this page: sensible estimation; accurate counting; making the five times table; observing the effect of multiplying by ten. The child may need help in all these areas. Note that many children have difficulty with accurate counting and can be shown that the strategy of grouping in fives can make the process easier. Once the table is complete discuss any patterns e.g. some answers are even some are odd. Can the child see why? Pay particular attention to 10 x 5 = 50. Point out that the number 5 in the answer is sitting in the tens column and that there is a 0 in the units column for that number. The child may notice that the five times table is special because there is always a five or a zero in the units column. You could extend the activity by showing the child numbers such as 100, which must be a multiple of five because it ends in a zero. If the child is gaining confidence you could suggest that s/he uses a calculator to find how many fives are in one hundred. This introduces a link between multiplication and division: 100 ÷ 5 = 20 because 20 x 5 = 100. You could continue this activity by showing numbers such as 345, 815, 720, etc, and by asking questions such as 'is 492 a multiple of five?'

Name: _____

Date: _____

How many hexagons do you think there are here?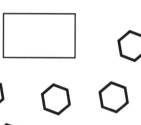

Now count the hexagons.

Draw rings around groups of six hexagons. Use these groups to help you to fill in the six times table.

1 x 6 = ☐ --------------------   6 x 6 = ☐ --------------------

2 x 6 = ☐ --------------------   7 x 6 = ☐ --------------------

3 x 6 = ☐ --------------------   8 x 6 = ☐ --------------------

4 x 6 = ☐ --------------------   9 x 6 = ☐ --------------------

5 x 6 = ☐ --------------------   10 x 6 = ☐ --------------------

Notes for teachers

Target: Solve one-step problems involving numbers, money or measures, including time; represent the information using numbers or diagrams; make and use tables to organise and interpret information; identify patterns or relationships involving numbers; describe and explain methods (Strand 1). Derive and recall multiplication facts (Strand 3). Multiply one-digit numbers by 10 (Strand 4).

There are several aspects to the work on this page: sensible estimation; accurate counting; making the six times table; observing the effect of multiplying by ten. The child may need help in all these areas. Note that many children have difficulty with accurate counting and can be shown that the strategy of grouping in sixes can make the process easier. Once the table is complete discuss any patterns e.g. all the answers are even numbers. Pay particular attention to 10 x 6 = 60. Ask the child to observe that the number 6 in the answer is sitting in the tens column and that there is a 0 in the units column for that number.

How many heptagons do you think there are here?

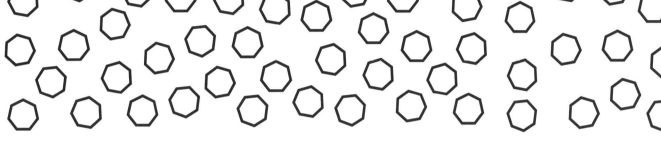

Now count the heptagons.

Draw rings around groups of seven heptagons. Use these groups to help you to fill in the seven times table.

1 x 7 = ☐ _____   6 x 7 = ☐ _____

2 x 7 = ☐ _____   7 x 7 = ☐ _____

3 x 7 = ☐ _____   8 x 7 = ☐ _____

4 x 7 = ☐ _____   9 x 7 = ☐ _____

5 x 7 = ☐ _____   10 x 7 = ☐ _____

Notes for teachers

Target: Solve one-step problems involving numbers, money or measures, including time; represent the information using numbers or diagrams; make and use tables to organise and interpret information; identify patterns or relationships involving numbers; describe and explain methods (Strand 1). Derive and recall multiplication facts (Strand 3). Multiply one-digit numbers by 10 (Strand 4).

There are several aspects to the work on this page: sensible estimation; accurate counting; making the three times table; observing the effect of multiplying by ten. The child may need support in all these areas. Note that many children have difficulty with accurate counting and can be shown that the strategy of grouping in sevens can make the process easier. Once the table is complete discuss any patterns e.g. some answers are even some are odd. Can the child see why? Pay particular attention to 10 x 7 = 70. Ask the child to observe that the number 7 in the answer is sitting in the tens column and that there is a 0 in the units column for that number.

Name: _____

Date: _____

How many octagons do you think there are here? [ ]

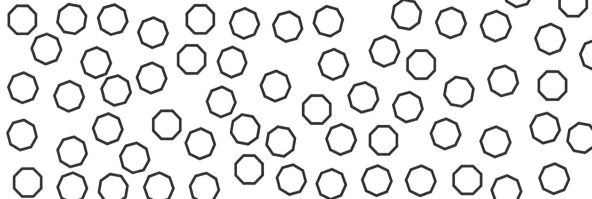

Now count the octagons.

Draw rings around groups of eight octagons. Use these groups to help you to fill in the eight times table.

1 x 8 = [ ] -----------------------
2 x 8 = [ ] -----------------------
3 x 8 = [ ] -----------------------
4 x 8 = [ ] -----------------------
5 x 8 = [ ] -----------------------

6 x 8 = [ ] -----------------------
7 x 8 = [ ] -----------------------
8 x 8 = [ ] -----------------------
9 x 8 = [ ] -----------------------
10 x 8 = [ ] -----------------------

Notes for teachers

Target: Solve one-step problems involving numbers, money or measures, including time; represent the information using numbers or diagrams; make and use tables to organise and interpret information; identify patterns or relationships involving numbers; describe and explain methods (Strand 1) Derive and recall multiplication facts (Strand 3). Multiply one-digit numbers by 10 (Strand 4).

There are several aspects to the work on this page: sensible estimation; accurate counting; making the eight times table; observing the effect of multiplying by ten. The child may need support in all these areas. Note that many children have difficulty with accurate counting and can be shown that the strategy of grouping in eights can make the process easier. Once the table is complete discuss any patterns e.g. all the answers are even numbers. Pay particular attention to 10 x 8 = 80. Point out that the number 8 in the answer is sitting in the tens column and that there is a 0 in the units column for that number. Looking at the digits in the unitís column shows the pattern 8, 6, 4, 2, 0, 8, 6, 4, 2, 0.

worksheet 34

How many circles do you think there are here?

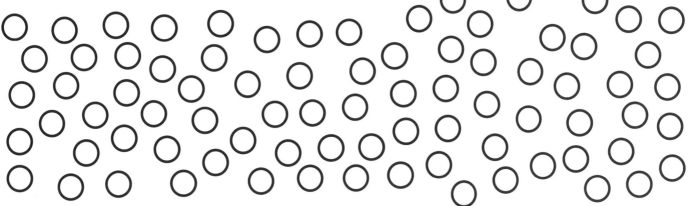

Now count the circles.

Draw rings around groups of nine circles. Use these groups to help you to fill in the nine times table.

1 x 9 =   _____

2 x 9 =   _____

3 x 9 =   _____

4 x 9 =   _____

5 x 9 =   _____

6 x 9 =   _____

7 x 9 =   _____

8 x 9 =   _____

9 x 9 =   _____

10 x 9 =   _____

Notes for teachers

Target: Solve one-step problems involving numbers, money or measures, including time; represent the information using numbers or diagrams; make and use tables to organise and interpret information; identify patterns or relationships involving numbers; describe and explain methods (Strand 1). Derive and recall multiplication facts (Strand 3). Multiply one-digit numbers by 10 (Strand 4).

There are several aspects to the work on this page: sensible estimation; accurate counting; making the nine times table; observing the effect of multiplying by ten. The child may need support in all these areas. Once the table is complete discuss any patterns e.g. some answers are even some are odd. Can the child see why? The child may observe that the tens column is empty for the first answer then goes up, 1 2 3 4 5 6 7 8 9, while the units column goes down 9 8 7 6 5 4 3 2 10. Another interesting feature of the nine times table is that the digits for each answer add up to 9. Pay particular attention to 10 x 9 = 90. Ask the child to observe that the number 9 in the answer is sitting in the tens column and that there is a 0 in the units column for that number.

Andrew Brodie: Supporting Maths © A & C Black Publishers Ltd. 2007

Name:

Date:

How many semi-circles do you think there are here?

Now count the semi-circles.

Draw rings around groups of ten semi-circles. Use these groups to help you to fill in the ten times table.

1 x 10 = ⬜ _____   6 x 10 = ⬜ _____

2 x 10 = ⬜ _____   7 x 10 = ⬜ _____

3 x 10 = ⬜ _____   8 x 10 = ⬜ _____

4 x 10 = ⬜ _____   9 x 10 = ⬜ _____

5 x 10 = ⬜ _____   10 x 10 = ⬜ _____

Notes for teachers

Target: Solve one-step problems involving numbers, money or measures, including time; represent the information using numbers or diagrams; make and use tables to organise and interpret information; identify patterns or relationships involving numbers; describe and explain methods (Strand 1). Derive and recall multiplication facts; recognise multiples of 10 up to 1000 (Strand 3). Multiply one-digit numbers by 10 (Strand 4).

There are several aspects to the work on this page: sensible estimation; accurate counting; making the ten times table; observing the effect of multiplying by ten. The child may need help in all these areas. Note that many children have difficulty with accurate counting and can be shown that the strategy of grouping in tens can make the process easier. Once the table is complete discuss any patterns e.g. all the answers are even numbers and end in zero. The child may identify the fact that the ten times table is special because there is always a zero in the units column. You could extend the activity by showing the child numbers such as 700, which must be a multiple of ten because it ends in a zero. If the child is gaining confidence you could suggest that s/he uses a calculator to find how many tens are in seven hundred – this reminds him/her of the link between multiplication and division: 700 ÷ 10 = 70 because 70 x 10 = 700 and 10 x 70 = 700. This activity provides an excellent opportunity for the child to practise multiplying any two-digit number by ten and observing the effect: s/he could use a calculator to multiply numbers such as 96 by 10 – s/he should be able to see that the 9 digit has moved from the tens column to the hundreds column, the 6 digit has moved from the units column to the tens column and the units column now has a 0. Try to discourage the child from saying 'you just add a nought'.

Name: **Date:**

How many twos are there in eight? ☐

$8 \div 2 =$ ☐

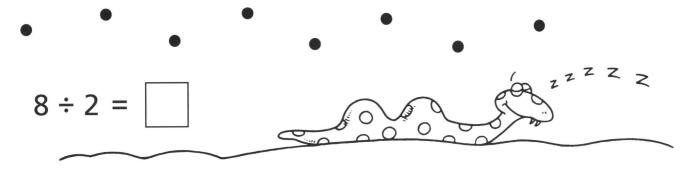

How much is eight shared between two? ☐

$8 \div 2 =$ ☐

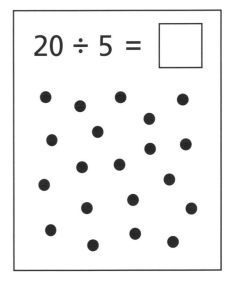

$12 \div 3 =$ ☐

$16 \div 8 =$ ☐

$20 \div 5 =$ ☐

Notes for teachers

Target: Solve one-step problems involving numbers, money or measures, including time; identify patterns or relationships involving numbers; describe and explain methods (Strand 1). Derive and recall multiplication facts and the corresponding division facts (Strand 3). Understand that division is the inverse of multiplication and vice versa (Strand 4).

The process of division can be very confusing for children, partly because it reflects two different situations: 'how many twos are there in eight?' is different from 'how much is eight shared between two?' although both give the same answer of four. When showing the child the second of the two questions using the dots above you may like to place counters on the dots to demonstrate the process of sharing the eight dots between the two of you. Having shown the child this process, return to the first example before supporting him/her in answering the remaining three questions using this method only.

Name: _____ **Date:** _____

18 ÷ 6 = ☐

24 ÷ 3 = ☐

15 ÷ 5 = ☐

30 ÷ 10 = ☐

28 ÷ 7 = ☐

32 ÷ 8 = ☐

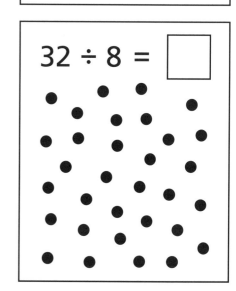

16 ÷ 4 = ☐

24 ÷ 8 = ☐

30 ÷ 5 = ☐

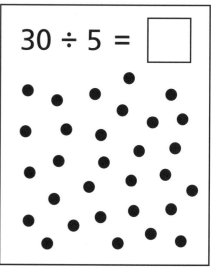

Notes for teachers

Target: Solve one-step problems involving numbers, money or measures, including time; identify patterns or relationships involving numbers; describe and explain methods (Strand 1). Derive and recall multiplication facts and the corresponding division facts (Strand 3). Understand that division is the inverse of multiplication and vice versa (Strand 4).

Before attempting this sheet ensure that the child has worked through Worksheet 36. Support her/him in answering each question by splitting the larger number into groups i.e. for the first question, ask the child 'how many sixes are there in eighteen?' S/he can draw rings around groups of six to find that there are three so 18 ÷ 6 = 3.

Name: _____   **Date:** _____

40 ÷ 5 = ☐

42 ÷ 7 = ☐

36 ÷ 9 = ☐

30 ÷ 2 = ☐

9 ÷ 3 = ☐

12 ÷ 4 = ☐

50 ÷ 10 = ☐

36 ÷ 4 = ☐

18 ÷ 9 = ☐

Notes for teachers

Target: Solve one-step problems involving numbers, money or measures, including time; identify patterns or relationships involving numbers; describe and explain methods (Strand 1). Derive and recall multiplication facts and the corresponding division facts (Strand 3). Understand that division is the inverse of multiplication and vice versa (Strand 4).

Before attempting this sheet ensure that the child has worked through Worksheet 36. Support her/him in answering each question by splitting the larger number into groups i.e. for the first question, ask the child 'how many fives are there in forty?' S/he can draw rings around groups of five to find that there are eight so 40 ÷ 5 = 8.

Name: _____   Date: _____

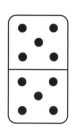
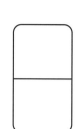
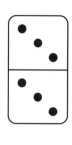
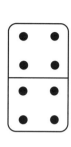
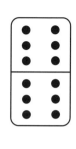
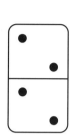

Double 5 = ☐	3 + 3 = ☐	2 x 6 = ☐
Double 3 = ☐	2 + 2 = ☐	2 x 0 = ☐
Double 6 = ☐	5 + 5 = ☐	2 x 3 = ☐
Double 2 = ☐	4 + 4 = ☐	2 x 1 = ☐
Double 1 = ☐	0 + 0 = ☐	2 x 2 = ☐
Double 0 = ☐	6 + 6 = ☐	2 x 5 = ☐
Double 4 = ☐	1 + 1 = ☐	2 x 4 = ☐
Double 9 = ☐	10 + 10 = ☐	2 x 8 = ☐
Double 8 = ☐	7 + 7 = ☐	2 x 10 = ☐
Double 10 = ☐	9 + 9 = ☐	2 x 7 = ☐
Double 7 = ☐	8 + 8 = ☐	2 x 9 = ☐

Notes for teachers

Target: Solve one-step problems involving numbers, money or measures, including time; identify patterns or relationships involving numbers; describe and explain methods (Strand 1). Derive and recall multiplication facts; use knowledge of number operations including doubling (Strand 3).

The child will be able to use the dominoes for help to answer the first seven questions in the left-hand column. Help her/him to recognise the links between the questions in the three columns by drawing lines between questions with the same answers. S/he can then attempt the final four questions in the lower three columns, again mapping the links by drawing lines.

Andrew Brodie: Supporting Maths © A & C Black Publishers Ltd. 2007

Name: _____   **Date:** _____

worksheet
40

What number is double two?
Count the birds in each set.

Double 2 = ☐

How many birds are there altogether?

What number is double twenty?   Double 20 = ☐

Now try these questions.

Double 30 = ☐   Double 60 = ☐   Double 50 = ☐

Double 10 = ☐   Double 80 = ☐   Double 40 = ☐

Double 90 = ☐   Double 70 = ☐   Double 100 = ☐

Notes for teachers
Target: Solve one-step problems involving numbers, money or measures, including time; identify patterns or relationships involving numbers; describe and explain methods (Strand 1). Derive and recall multiplication facts; use knowledge of number operations including doubling (Strand 3).
Help the child to recognise the link between double 2 and double 20, and then to complete all the other doubles. As an extension activity, before introducing Worksheet 41, ask the child if s/he can find double 21. Help her/him to double 20, then double 1, then add the two answers together.

Name: _____ **Date:** _____

What number is double twenty-six?

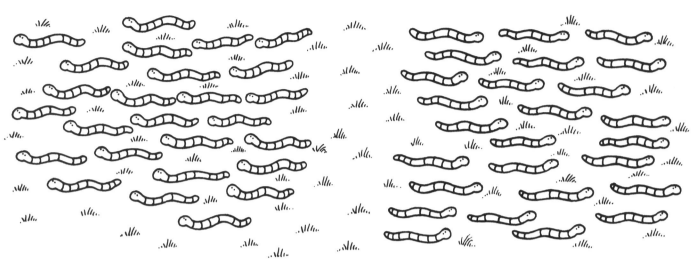

Step 1
Find double 20

Double 20 = ☐

Step 2
Find double 6

Double 6 = ☐

Step 3:
Add the two answers together

☐ + ☐ = ☐

Now try these questions.

Double 23 = ☐   Double 32 = ☐   Double 44 = ☐

Double 15 = ☐   Double 17 = ☐   Double 51 = ☐

Double 63 = ☐   Double 37 = ☐   Double 99 = ☐

Notes for teachers
Target: Solve one-step problems involving numbers, money or measures, including time; identify patterns or relationships involving numbers; describe and explain methods (Strand 1). Derive and recall multiplication facts; use knowledge of number operations including doubling (Strand 3).
Help the child to work through the example of double 26 and then to answer the other questions in the same way. Discuss the answers with the child, particularly double 51 as the answer is close to 100 and double 99 as the answer is close to 200.

Andrew Brodie: Supporting Maths © A & C Black Publishers Ltd. 2007

How many spots are there altogether on each domino?

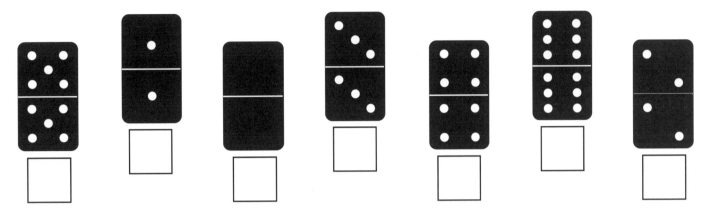

Half of 10 = ☐

10 ÷ 2 = ☐

Half of 2 = ☐

2 ÷ 2 = ☐

Half of 12 = ☐

12 ÷ 2 = ☐

Half of 6 = ☐

6 ÷ 2 = ☐

Half of 8 = ☐

8 ÷ 2 = ☐

Half of 4 = ☐

4 ÷ 2 = ☐

Now try these questions.

Half of 18 = ☐

18 ÷ 2 = ☐

Half of 20 = ☐

20 ÷ 2 = ☐

Half of 14 = ☐

14 ÷ 2 = ☐

Half of 16 = ☐

16 ÷ 2 = ☐

Notes for teachers

Target: Solve one-step problems involving numbers, money or measures, including time; identify patterns or relationships involving numbers; describe and explain methods (Strand 1). Derive and recall multiplication facts; use knowledge of number operations including doubling and halving (Strand 3). Find unit fractions of numbers (Strand 4).

The child will be able to use the dominoes to help answer the questions in the first set. Help her/him to realise that halving is the same as sharing between two. In discussing the final question in the first set of questions, remind the child that half of zero is zero, double zero is zero, zero times any number is always zero. Help the child to answer the questions in the second set. If necessary you could use counters e.g. for the first question ask the child to collect 18 counters then to share these into two piles.

Name:

Date:

Match the questions to the answers.

1	
Half of 10	3
Half of 4	2
Half of 12	5
Half of 6	4
Half of 2	6
Half of 8	1

Now try these.

2	
Half of 20	7
Half of 14	9
Half of 18	8
Half of 16	10

Now try these.

3	
Half of 10	15
Half of 20	20
Half of 30	25
Half of 40	5
Half of 50	10
Half of 60	50
Half of 70	45
Half of 80	25
Half of 90	30
Half of 100	35

Notes for teachers

Target: Solve one-step problems involving numbers, money or measures, including time; identify patterns or relationships involving numbers; describe and explain methods (Strand 1). Derive and recall multiplication facts; use knowledge of number operations including doubling and halving (Strand 3). Find unit fractions of numbers (Strand 4).

Check that the child has completed Worksheet 42 before attempting this sheet. The first two sets of questions on this sheet provide additional practice of those on Worksheet 42. The child will be able to find the answers to the first two questions in the final set as s/he has met the questions already and s/he will probably be able to find the answers to 'half of 40', 'half of 60', 'half of 80' and 'half of 100' quite easily. The other questions are more difficult but can be solved by using information from the other answers e.g. if the child knows that half of 20 is 10 and that half of 40 is 20 then s/he may be able to work out that half of 30 is midway between 10 and 20, i.e. 15.

Name: _____ **Date:** _____

half $\dfrac{1}{2}$

quarter $\dfrac{1}{4}$

three quarters $\dfrac{3}{4}$

Write the correct fraction and the correct fraction words for each shape. The first one has been done for you.

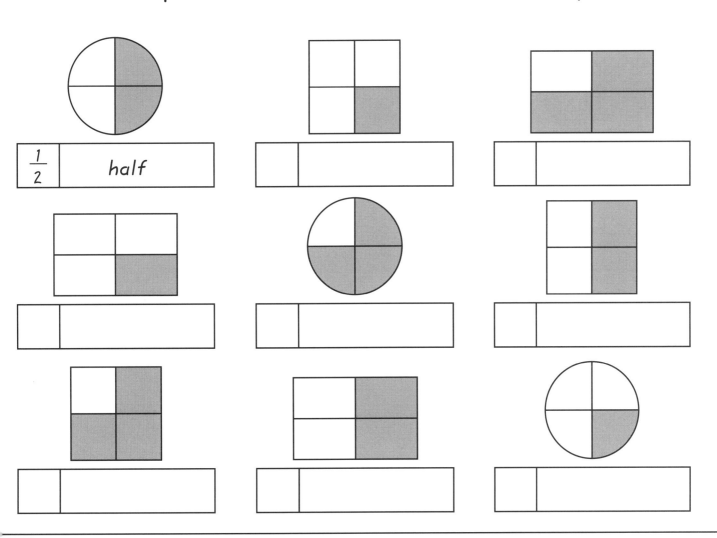

$\dfrac{1}{2}$	half

Notes for teachers

Target: Solve one-step problems involving numbers, money or measures, including time; identify patterns or relationships involving numbers; describe and explain methods (Strand 1). Read and write proper fractions interpreting the denominator as the parts of a whole and the numerator as the number of parts; identify and estimate fractions of shapes; use diagrams to compare fractions (Strand 2).

Look at the fractions with the child as both words and mathematical symbols before looking at the shapes. The child will probably be able to identify the half shapes very easily but it is still worth discussing these. Point out that the two at the bottom of the fraction is called the denominator and it shows that the shape has been cut into two pieces, and the one at the top is called the numerator and shows the number of pieces we are looking at i.e. one piece out of two. This becomes more obvious when looking at the shapes that are shaded to show three quarters. If you feel that the child is confident you could extend the activity by drawing a shape marked in quarters then demonstrating that two quarters is equivalent to a half.

Name: Date:

half	$\frac{1}{2}$	one third	$\frac{1}{3}$	two fifths	$\frac{2}{5}$
quarter	$\frac{1}{4}$	two thirds	$\frac{2}{3}$	three fifths	$\frac{3}{5}$
three quarters	$\frac{3}{4}$	one fifth	$\frac{1}{5}$	four fifths	$\frac{4}{5}$

Write the correct fraction and the correct fraction words for each shape. The first one has been done for you.

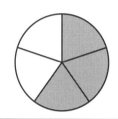
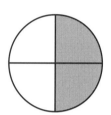
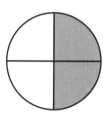

$\frac{3}{5}$ three fifths

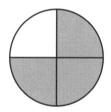
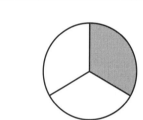
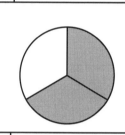

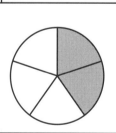
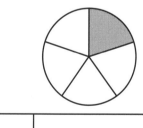
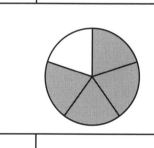

Notes for teachers

Target: Solve one-step problems involving numbers, money or measures, including time; identify patterns or relationships involving numbers; describe and explain methods (Strand 1). Read and write proper fractions interpreting the denominator as the parts of a whole and the numerator as the number of parts; identify and estimate fractions of shapes; use diagrams to compare fractions (Strand 2).

Help the child read both words and mathematical symbols before looking at the shapes. Look at the first shape with the child reminding her/him that the bottom of the fraction is called the denominator and it shows that the shape has been cut into five pieces, and the one at the top is called the numerator and shows the number of pieces we are looking at i.e. three pieces out of five.

Name: **Date:**

This number is eight:
units
8

This number is eighty:
tens   units
8   0

When 8 is multiplied by 10 it moves into the tens column and the units column has a zero.

$$10 \times 8 = 80$$

This number is forty three:
tens   units
4   3

This number is four hundred and thirty:
hundreds   tens   units
4   3   0

When 43 is multiplied by 10 the four moves into the hundreds column, the three moves into the tens column and the units column has a zero.

$$10 \times 43 = 430$$

Now try these:

$10 \times 5 =$ ☐ $10 \times 81 =$ ☐ $10 \times 1 =$ ☐

$10 \times 32 =$ ☐ $10 \times 17 =$ ☐ $10 \times 48 =$ ☐

$10 \times 6 =$ ☐ $10 \times 27 =$ ☐ $10 \times 99 =$ ☐

Now try these:

$4 \times 10 =$ ☐ $8 \times 10 =$ ☐ $51 \times 10 =$ ☐

$25 \times 10 =$ ☐ $74 \times 10 =$ ☐ $82 \times 10 =$ ☐

$66 \times 10 =$ ☐ $36 \times 10 =$ ☐ $99 \times 10 =$ ☐

Notes for teachers

Target: Solve one-step problems involving numbers, money or measures, including time; represent the information using numbers or diagrams; make and use tables to organise and interpret information; identify patterns or relationships involving numbers; describe and explain methods (Strand 1). Derive and recall multiplication facts; recognise multiples of 10 up to 1000 (Strand 3). Multiply one-digit and two-digit numbers by 10 (Strand 4).

Discuss the two examples with the child drawing attention to what happens to the digits when the numbers are multiplied by ten. Try to discourage the child from saying 'you just add a nought'. (Please note that mathematically 'eight multiplied by ten' should be written '8 x 10' rather than '10 x 8'. However, we are showing the format traditionally used on multiplication tables). Help the child where necessary with the questions. Some are set out like this: 10 x 5 and some like this: 4 x 10 and you should explain to the child that the effect is the same in both cases. S/he may notice that the final question in each set produces the same answer.

Name: _____ **Date:** _____

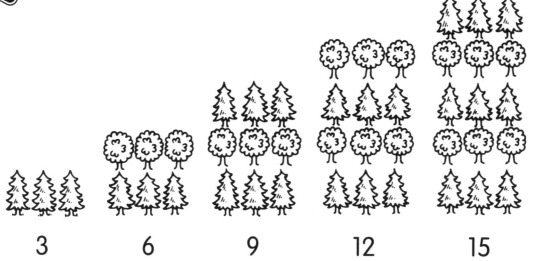

3   6   9   12   15   …

This is called a number sequence: 3, 6, 9, 12, 15, …

What is the next number
in the sequence? ☐   …and the next number? ☐

Look at the number sequences below. Write two more
numbers for each one.

8,	10,	12,	14,	16,	☐	☐
5,	10,	15,	20,	25,	☐	☐
17,	19,	21,	23,	25,	☐	☐
8,	11,	14,	17,	20,	☐	☐
24,	22,	20,	18,	16,	☐	☐

Notes for teachers

Target: Solve one-step problems involving numbers, money or measures, including time, choosing and carrying out appropriate calculations; follow a line of enquiry by deciding what information is important; identify patterns or relationships involving numbers; describe and explain methods (Strand 1). Recognise and continue number sequences formed by counting on or back in steps of constant size (Strand 2). Add or subtract mentally combinations of one-digit and two-digit numbers (Strand 4).

Discuss the example sequence with the child, identifying the fact that the numbers are increasing by three and finding the two missing numbers. When the child approaches the questions you could suggest that s/he draws a small arrow between each pair of numbers and labels the arrow with the value that is being added or subtracted e.g. 8, ₊₂ 10, ₊₂ 12, ₊₂ 14, ₊₂ 16,

Andrew Brodie: Supporting Maths © A & C Black Publishers Ltd. 2007

Use your ruler to measure these lines to the nearest half centimetre. The first two lines have been measured for you.

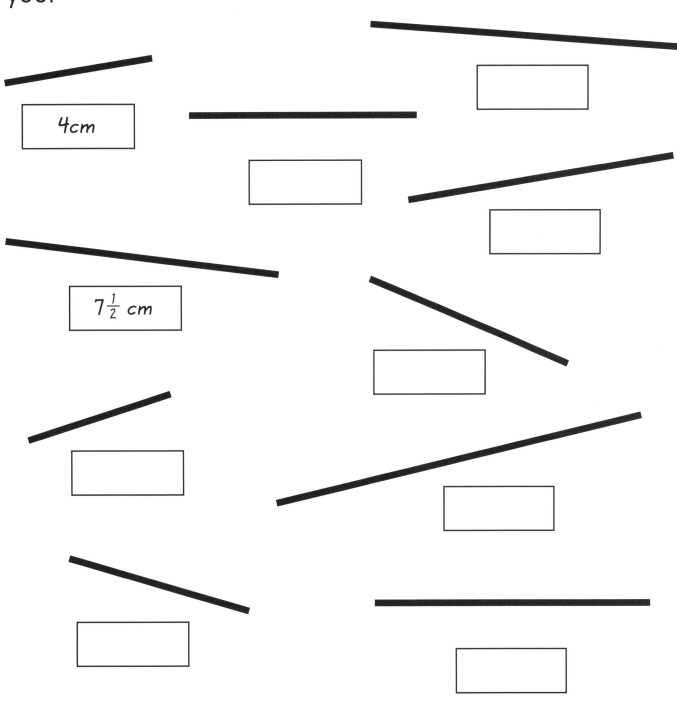

4cm

$7\frac{1}{2}$ cm

Notes for teachers
Target: Solve one-step problems involving numbers, money or measures; follow a line of enquiry by deciding what information is important; describe and explain methods (Strand 1). Read, to the nearest division and half-division, scales that are numbered or partially numbered; use the information to measure and draw to a suitable degree of accuracy (Strand 6). Examine the child's ruler with her/him, ensuring that s/he can identify the centimetre and half-centimetre markings. Help her/him to measure the first line to confirm that, to the nearest half centimetre, it is 4cm long. Look at the second line in the same way then ask the child to measure the other lines. Check that s/he is measuring from the zero mark and not from the very end of the ruler. As an extension activity you could ask the child to draw some lines to lengths that you specify.
Andrew Brodie: Supporting Maths © A & C Black Publishers Ltd. 2007
53

Name: **Date:**

This is Arnold the Ant.
Find how far Arnold has to walk to get round each
rectangle. The first one has been done for you.

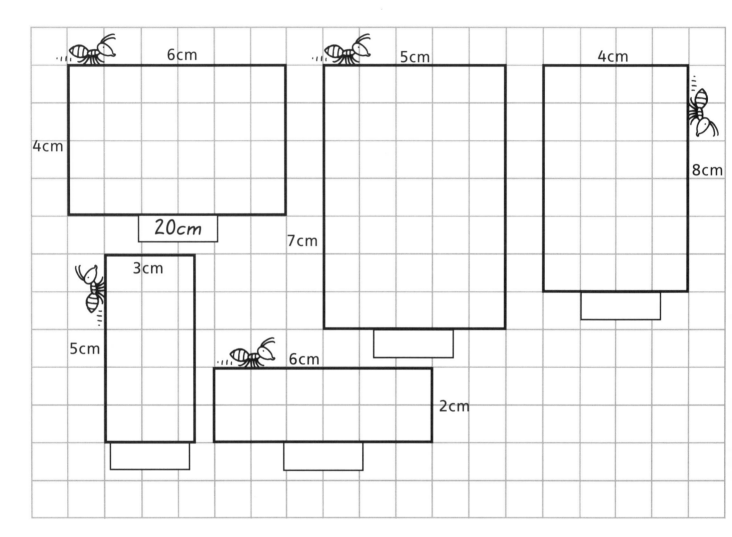

The distance all the way round is called the perimeter
of the rectangle.
You have found the perimeter of each rectangle.
Draw your own rectangle on the grid then find its perimeter.

Notes for teachers
Target: Solve one-step problems involving numbers, money or measures, choosing and carrying out appropriate
calculations; follow a line of enquiry by deciding what information is important; describe and explain methods (Strand 1).
Choose and use standard metric units and their abbreviations when estimating, measuring and recording length; draw
rectangles and measure and calculate their perimeters (Strand 6).
Check that the child understands that perimeter refers to the distance around the rectangle. S/he can find each perimeter
by counting centimetres all the way round each shape but s/he could also use addition by, for example, completing
6 + 4 + 6 + 4 for the first shape. Finding the perimeter can be demonstrated by using a ruler and measuring each side,
instead of counting the edges of the squares – this avoids the situation where a child is counting the squares themselves
rather than the edges.

          Andrew Brodie: Supporting Maths © A & C Black Publishers Ltd. 2007

Name:

Date:

Measuring areas of rectangles
This is Arnold the Ant.
Count the squares to find out how much space Arnold has
in each rectangle. The first one has been done for you.

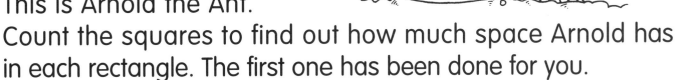

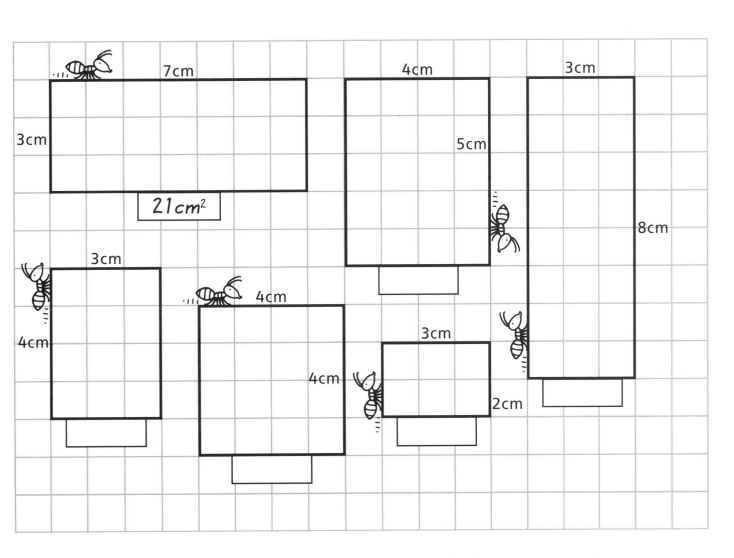

The space inside is called the area of the rectangle.
You have found the area of each rectangle.

Notes for teachers

Target: Solve one-step problems involving numbers, money or measures, choosing and carrying out appropriate
calculations; follow a line of enquiry by deciding what information is important; describe and explain methods (Strand 1).
Choose and use standard metric units and their abbreviations when estimating, measuring and recording length; find the
area of rectilinear shapes drawn on a square grid by counting squares (Strand 6).
Many children confuse perimeter with area. Help them to understand that area measures the amount of space covered
and can be found by counting squares, whereas the perimeter measures the distance around a shape and is found by
counting the sides of squares.

Name: **Date:**

Complete each picture by drawing the reflection of the part shown.

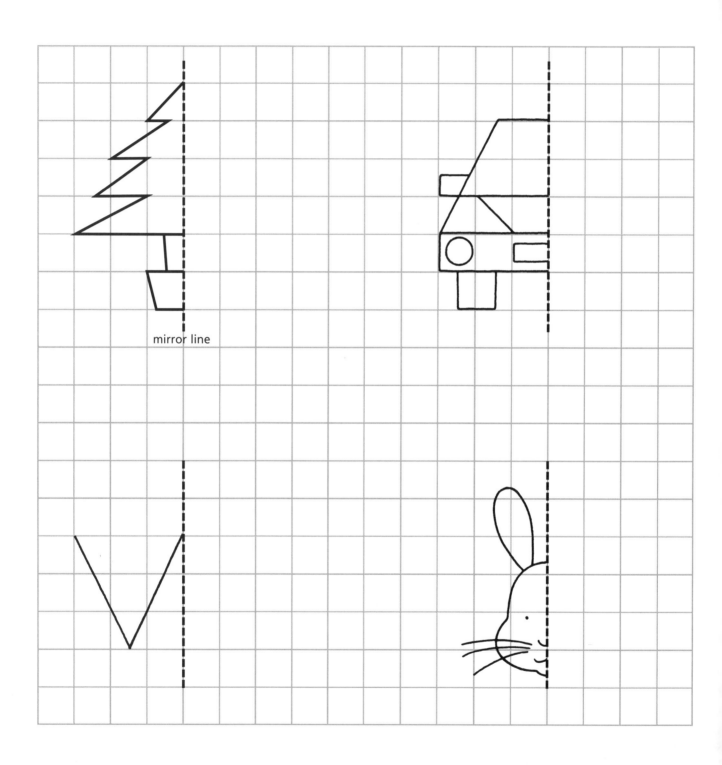

mirror line

Notes for teachers

Target: Solve one-step problems involving numbers, money or measures; follow a line of enquiry by deciding what information is important; describe and explain methods (Strand 1). Draw and complete shapes with reflective symmetry; draw the reflection of a shape in a mirror line along one side (Strand 5).
Help the child to identify key points in each picture then to measure or count out to these points from the mirror line. To create these points in the reflected part of the picture s/he can then count out from the mirror line in the opposite direction.

Listen carefully to your teacher.

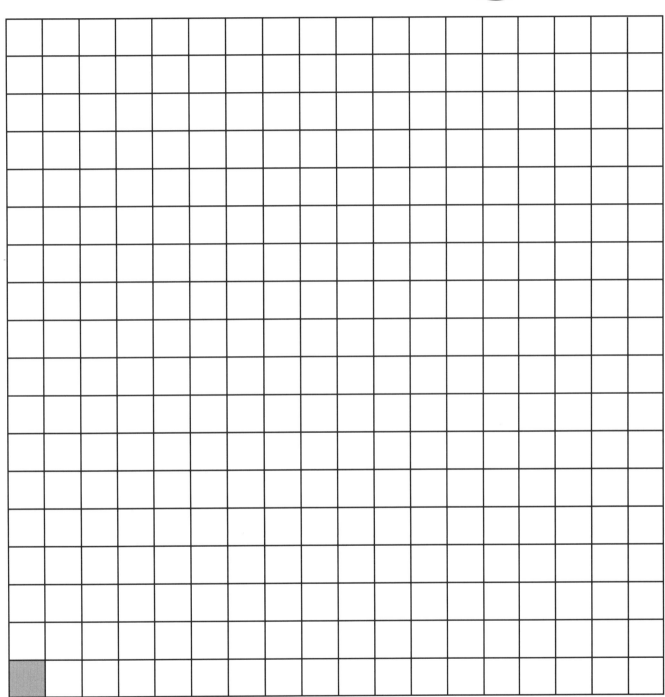

Notes for teachers

Target: Solve one-step problems involving numbers, money or measures; follow a line of enquiry by deciding what information is important; describe and explain methods (Strand 1). Use the four compass points to describe movement about a grid (Strand 5).

You may like to photocopy this worksheet twice: one copy for the child to fill in by following your instructions as detailed below and one for you to fill in by following the childís instructions. Ask the child to start by drawing a dot in the middle of the shaded square then to draw a line from the dot moving the pencil 9cm towards the East, then 10cm North, 2cm West, 2cm South, 3cm East, 3cm North, 4cm West etc, creating a spiral pattern. Then allow the child to give you instructions to create a picture or pattern on your sheet.

Listen carefully to your teacher.

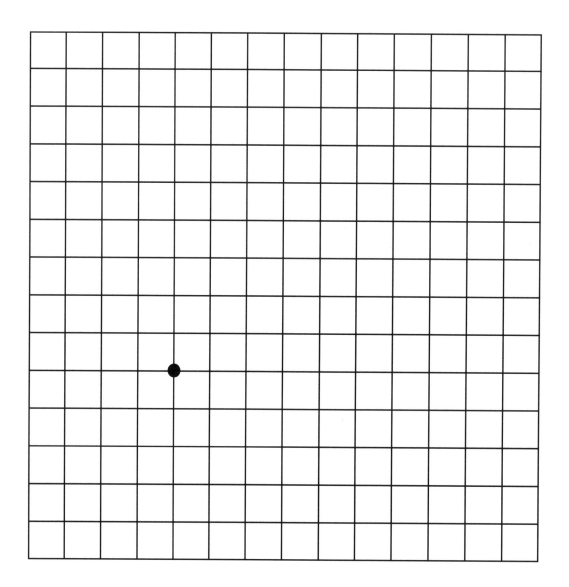

Notes for teachers

Target: Solve one-step problems involving numbers, money or measures; follow a line of enquiry by deciding what information is important; describe and explain methods (Strand 1). Use the four compass points to describe movement about a grid (Strand 5).

You may like to photocopy this worksheet twice: one copy for the child to fill in by following your instructions as detailed below and one for you to fill in by following the child's instructions. Ask the child to start at the dot and then to draw lines as follows: across three squares in a South-East direction, along three squares in an East direction, across three squares in a North-East direction, up three squares in a North direction, across three squares in a North-West direction, along three squares in a West direction, across three squares in a South-West direction then down three squares in a South direction. Can the child identify the shape that s/he has drawn? It should be an octagon. As an extension to this activity you could take the child outside with a compass and give instructions for moving about the playground a specified number of steps in particular directions. S/he could then give you instructions.

Name: _____ **Date:** _____

Make a right angle measurer.

This is a
right angle.

Take a piece of
scrap paper.

Fold it in half

Fold it again.

Use your right angle measurer to measure these angles.
Put a tick by the angle if it is a right angle.
Write bigger if it is bigger than a right angle.
Write smaller if it is smaller than a right angle.

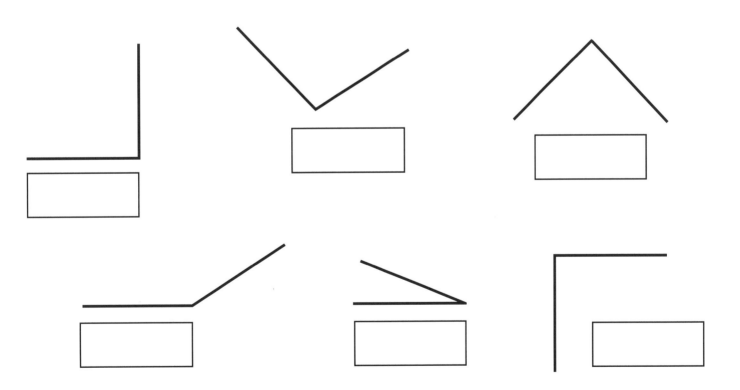

Notes for teachers

Target: Solve one-step problems involving numbers, money or measures; follow a line of enquiry by deciding what information is important; describe and explain methods (Strand 1). Compare angles with a right angle (Strand 5).
Help the child to fold the scrap paper carefully to make a sharp edge and to fold this edge exactly on itself to make a right angle. Help her/him to use this right angle to compare with the angles on the sheet. S/he should hold the right angle measurer against one line of each angle so that the point of the measurer matches the point of the angle. If the other line is not visible the angle is smaller than a right angle. If it appears exactly alongside the angle measurer then the angle is a right angle. If it is away from the angle measurer it must be bigger than a right angle.

Andrew Brodie: Supporting Maths © A & C Black Publishers Ltd. 2007

Find the right place for your shapes in this Venn diagram.

has 4 sides

has at least one right angle

Notes for teachers

Target: Represent the information in a puzzle or problem using diagrams; follow a line of enquiry by deciding what information is important; identify patterns and relationships involving shapes and use these to solve problems; describe and explain methods, choices and solutions to puzzles and problems, orally and in writing, using pictures and diagrams (Strand 1). Relate 2-D shapes to drawings of them; describe and classify the shapes (Strand 5). Use Venn or Carroll diagrams to sort data and objects using more than one criterion (Strand 7).

You could photocopy and laminate Resource sheets A and B from the back of this book to use with this worksheet. Alternatively, you could ask the child to cut out the shapes from the Resource sheets, discussing them and identifying them as s/he does so. Present the child with the collection of shapes then support her/him in finding the shapes with four sides that can fit into the left circle of the Venn diagram. Now help the child sort through all the other shapes finding those with right angles that will fit into the right circle. Ask the child to find the shapes with right angles from the set of four-sided shapes. They will, hopefully, identify the squares and the rectangles and will place them in the overlap of the diagram.

Andrew Brodie: Supporting Maths © A & C Black Publishers Ltd. 2007

Name: Date:

Find the right place for your shapes in this Venn diagram.

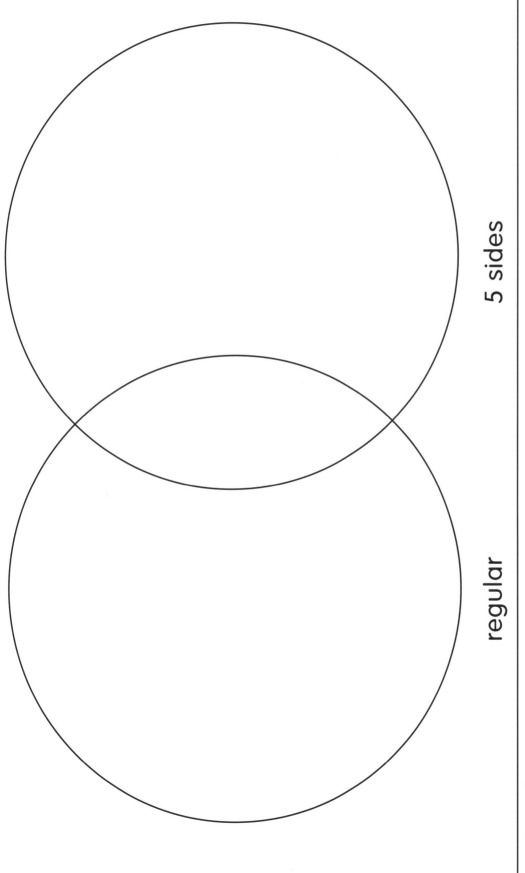

5 sides

regular

Notes for teachers

Target: Represent the information in a puzzle or problem using diagrams; follow a line of enquiry by deciding what information is important; identify patterns and relationships involving shapes and use these to solve problems; describe and explain methods, choices and solutions to puzzles and problems, orally and in writing, using pictures and diagrams (Strand 1). Relate 2-D shapes to drawings of them; describe and classify the shapes (Strand 5). Use Venn or Carroll diagrams to sort data and objects using more than one criterion (Strand 7).

You could photocopy and laminate Resource sheets A and B from the back of this book to use with this worksheet. Alternatively, you could ask the child to cut out the shapes from the Resource sheets, discussing them and identifying them as s/he does so. Present the child with the collection of shapes then help her/him sort them according to the criteria shown on the diagram. S/he should find several shapes to fit in the left circle, two pentagons to fit in the right circle with the regular pentagon fitting in the overlap.

A Carroll diagram

	right angles	no right angles
4 sides		
3 sides		

Notes for teachers

Target: Represent the information in a puzzle or problem using diagrams; follow a line of enquiry by deciding what information is important; identify patterns and relationships involving shapes and use these to solve problems; describe and explain methods, choices and solutions to puzzles and problems, orally and in writing, using pictures and diagrams (Strand 1). Relate 2-D shapes to drawings of them; describe and classify the shapes (Strand 5). Use Venn or Carroll diagrams to sort data and objects using more than one criterion (Strand 7).

You could photocopy and laminate Resource sheets A and B from the back of this book to use with this worksheet. Alternatively, you could ask the child to cut out the shapes from the Resource sheets, discussing them and identifying them as s/he does so. Present the child with the collection of shapes then help her/him to sort them according to the criteria shown on the diagram. As with the Venn diagrams this activity provides lots of opportunities for speaking and listening and for developing a logical approach to problem solving.

Resource sheet A